MASSACHUSETTS DRIVER'S MANUAL 2024

Drive Smart, Drive Safe A Complete Resource with 160 DMV Practice Questions

HEATHER ADAMS

Copyrighted Material

© 2024 Heather Adams

All rights reserved. No part of this book may be reproduced, distributed, or transmitted in any form or by any means, including photocopying, recording, or other electronic or mechanical methods, without the prior written permission of the publisher, except in the case of brief quotations embodied in critical reviews and certain other noncommercial uses permitted by copyright law.

Copyrighted Material

TABLE OF CONTENTS

INTRODUCTION..5
    Welcome Note..5
    Purpose of the Manual..7
    Overview of Massachusetts Driving Regulations......9

CHAPTER 1: GETTING STARTED............................12
    Understanding the Massachusetts Driver's Manual 12
    Obtaining a Copy..15
    Navigating the Manual Effectively............................18

CHAPTER 2: THE LICENSING PROCESS................22
    Types of Licenses..22
    Eligibility Requirements...25
    Application Procedures...31
    Learner's Permit Restrictions...................................37

CHAPTER 3: RULES OF THE ROAD........................42
    Traffic Signs and Signals..42
    Right of Way..47
    Speed Limits..52
    Lane Usage and Changes..56

CHAPTER 4: SAFE DRIVING PRACTICES...............61
    Defensive Driving Techniques..................................61
    Handling Intersections..65
    Sharing the Road with Pedestrians and Bicyclists..69
    Adverse Weather Conditions....................................74

CHAPTER 5: VEHICLE OPERATION........................79
    Vehicle Controls and Instruments............................79
    Basic Vehicle Maintenance......................................83

    Handling Emergencies...88
    Driving in Construction Zones................................94
CHAPTER 6: SPECIAL DRIVING CONDITIONS......100
    Night Driving Safety Tips... 100
    Driving in Fog or Heavy Rain................................105
    Navigating Hills and Curves................................. 110
    Railroad Crossings...115
CHAPTER 7: MASSACHUSETTS TRAFFIC LAWS.120
    DUI/DWI Laws in Massachusetts........................ 120
    Seat Belts and Child Restraint Laws................... 126
    Mobile Phone and Texting Regulations................ 130
    Parking Regulations..134
CHAPTER 8: DRIVER'S RESPONSIBILITIES..........140
    Reporting Accidents...140
    Insurance Requirements.......................................143
    Understanding Points and Penalties....................147
    Handling Traffic Tickets....................................... 150
CHAPTER 9: COMMERCIAL DRIVER'S LICENSE (CDL)..154
    Overview of CDL Requirements........................... 154
    Endorsements and Restrictions for Commercial Drivers Licenses (CDL)...157
    CDL Test Procedures...161
    Safety Regulations for Commercial Drivers..........165
CHAPTER 10: ADDITIONAL RESOURCES.............170
    Useful Websites and Contact Information............ 170
    Glossary of Terms..173
    Practice Tests and Study Tips.............................. 182
APPENDIX: SAMPLE TEST QUESTIONS................190

Copyrighted Material

Multiple-Choice Questions.....................................190
Scenario-Based Questions...................................194
Answers and Explanations.................................. 197
CONCLUSION.. **204**

INTRODUCTION

Welcome to the Massachusetts Driving Regulations Manual – comprehensive guide for navigating the roads and understanding driving rules in the Bay State. Whether you're a new resident, visitor, or a seasoned driver, this manual provides essential information for safe driving in Massachusetts.

Welcome Note

Dear Reader,

Welcome to the vibrant world of Massachusetts driving, where each journey unfolds as a unique story. Whether you're a first-time driver, a newcomer to our picturesque state, or a seasoned road explorer, we warmly invite you into the realm of Bay State driving.

Envision roads winding through historic towns, coastal highways with breathtaking views, and city streets pulsating with energy. Massachusetts driving is not just a means of transportation; it's a dynamic experience, inviting you to be part of a community valuing safety, courtesy, and the joy of exploration.

In the Massachusetts Driver's Manual 2024, you'll find more than just rules and regulations; you'll discover the essence of driving in our state. It's about connections at intersections, shared moments on scenic routes, and the responsibility for fellow travelers' well-being.

Whether you're a new driver or refreshing your knowledge, consider this welcome a handshake from Massachusetts' diverse driving community. Embrace the roads, respect fellow drivers, and savor the beauty of landscapes that make each journey uniquely Bay State.

Safe travels, and welcome to Massachusetts' open roads!

Purpose of the Manual

This manual is crafted to ensure a comprehensive understanding of Massachusetts driving regulations, catering to both new and experienced drivers. Our goal is to cultivate a community of informed drivers who not only comply with the law but also contribute to a safer and more efficient traffic environment.

- **Informed Decision-Making:** Beyond surface-level regulations, this manual aims to empower drivers, novice and experienced alike, with in-depth insights into Massachusetts roadway rules. The goal is to enable you to make informed decisions while behind the wheel.

- **Promoting Responsible Driving:** More than guidelines, this manual acts as a catalyst for fostering responsible driving habits. We believe that an informed driver is a safer driver, contributing to a positive and secure driving environment. Each chapter is a roadmap to becoming a conscientious and courteous driver.

- **Community Well-Being:** This manual reflects our commitment to the well-being of Massachusetts' driving community. By promoting understanding and adherence to driving regulations, we enhance overall road safety and efficiency. Every driver plays a crucial role in shaping driving culture, and this manual is your guide to being a responsible participant in that collective effort.

- **A Reference for All Drivers:** Whether obtaining your first license or refreshing your knowledge as an experienced driver, this manual is tailored to your needs. It's more than an exam guide; it's a valuable resource for every journey, providing clarity on regulations, answering queries, and boosting confidence on the road.

As you delve into the **Massachusetts Driver's Manual 2024**, remember it's not just a set of rules – it's the key to unlocking a world of safe, informed, and enjoyable driving experiences. I hope your travels bring you as much joy as your final destination. Safe travels.

Overview of Massachusetts Driving Regulations

Welcome to the heart of the Massachusetts Driver's Manual 2024—an insightful journey into the regulations shaping the diverse landscapes of the Bay State. This overview serves as your compass, offering a glimpse into the rules governing your travels through Massachusetts's charming streets, bustling highways, and scenic byways.

- **Navigating the Rule Tapestry:** Envision the roadways unfolding, each governed by regulations ensuring safety, order, and smooth traffic flow. This overview is your entry point into this intricate tapestry, providing a preliminary understanding of the driving landscape awaiting exploration.

- **Diverse Driving Environments:** Massachusetts features a rich variety of driving environments—from vibrant urban centers to tranquil rural roads. Different regulations come into play, contributing to the unique character of the Bay State's roads. This overview provides a glimpse into the nuances of regulations tailored to these various driving scenarios.

- **Foundations of Safe Driving:** Get a brief preview of the foundational elements underscoring safe driving in Massachusetts. From traffic signs and right-of-way principles to speed limits and safe driving practices, this overview sets the stage for a deeper exploration of essential rules defining responsible driving behavior.

- **Cultivating Informed Drivers:** Consider this overview as a roadmap, guiding you to a comprehensive understanding of Massachusetts driving regulations. By providing a sneak peek into the rules shaping the driving experience, we aim to cultivate informed drivers—individuals who not only abide by the regulations but contribute to a collective commitment to safety and responsible driving.

As you delve into the **Massachusetts Driver's Manual 2024**, let this overview be your starting point—a gateway to a world of knowledge enhancing your driving journey through the picturesque roads of Massachusetts. Safe travels!

CHAPTER 1: GETTING STARTED

Welcome to Chapter 1, where we will reveal the crucial steps to begin your journey into the world of Massachusetts driving. Consider this chapter your compass, guiding you through the essentials of using the Massachusetts Driver's Manual 2024.

Understanding the Massachusetts Driver's Manual

Welcome to a deep dive into the Massachusetts Driver's Manual. This section aims to unravel the manual's main components and structure, providing you with a solid foundation as you continue on your journey to becoming a successful driver in the Bay State.

- **Overview of Contents:** Understanding the manual requires an understanding of its contents. Each chapter is meticulously crafted to clarify crucial aspects of

Massachusetts driving regulations. From the foundations of obtaining a license to the complexity of particular driving circumstances, each topic is a building block that contributes to your overall understanding.

- **Organization and flow:** Knowing how the manual is organized allows you to easily go through it. The chapters are organized methodically, guiding you through the learning process progressively. This structured flow ensures that you build on your knowledge step by step as you go through the manual.
- **Visual aids and examples:** Visual aids and real-world examples may help you comprehend more clearly. From traffic sign images to scenario-based explanations, these features are strategically placed to supplement the textual information. Accept them as valuable instruments for making

complex laws more tangible and understandable.

- **Key Terms and Definitions:** Familiarize yourself with key terminologies before beginning to read the book. A dedicated glossary provides detailed explanations, ensuring that you understand the language used throughout the manual. Understanding these terms is critical for interpreting rules successfully.

- **Interactive elements:** This manual is not a one-way street. Throughout the chapters, interactive elements such as practice questions and scenarios encourage active participation. Treat them as checkpoints to assess your progress and solidify your knowledge before hitting the road.

As you study the Massachusetts Driver's Manual, consider this section to be your orientation to the journey ahead. Mastering its structure provides you with the ability to traverse the complex network of rules that govern Massachusetts' roadways. So, fasten your seatbelts and join us on this journey to enlightenment.

Obtaining a Copy

Congratulations on taking the first step in mastering Massachusetts driving standards. Before we continue on this journey, let's investigate the many channels accessible for getting a copy of the Massachusetts Driver's Manual. Choose the strategy that best suits your preferences and learning style.

- **Online Download:** In the digital era, convenience is readily accessible. To get a digital copy of the manual, visit the official Massachusetts Registry of Motor Vehicles (RMV) website. This alternative gives immediate access, allowing you to begin your learning journey without delay.
- **Physical copies from the RMV offices:** Do you prefer a tactile book? Head to your

nearest RMV office to pick up a physical copy. The offices are strategically placed around the state, making it easy for you to get a manual in person. Having a physical copy may be particularly useful for those who like flipping over pages and taking notes.
- **Driver Education Programs:** If you're enrolled in a driver's education program, consult your instructor or the program coordinator. Many driver's education programs provide students with a copy of the manual as part of the curriculum. It's a simple option for those taking certified driving lessons.
- **Third-Party Vendors:** Investigate the possibility of acquiring a copy from third-party retailers. Copies of the Massachusetts Driver's Manual may be available in bookstores, online retailers, and educational supply stores. Keep in mind that

availability may vary, so check with local merchants or look into online platforms for options.

- **Local Libraries:** For those who appreciate the appeal of libraries can inquire about the availability of the manual at their local library. Some libraries have educational materials, and you may find a copy available for borrowing. It is a cost-effective option for those who do not want to purchase a copy.

As you begin your journey to understand Massachusetts driving rules, choose the approach that best suits your interests. Whether you pick a digital download, a physical copy, or an educational program resource, the main thing is to have your manual ready as your trusted companion on the way to becoming an educated and responsible driver. Travel safely on this learning adventure!

Navigating the Manual Effectively

As you delve into the Massachusetts Driver's Manual, mastering effective navigation is crucial to enhance your learning experience. Here are tips to seamlessly explore the manual and locate the information you need:

- **Utilize the Table of Contents:** Start with the Table of Contents as your guide. It provides an organized overview of the manual's contents. Identify your specific topic of interest and use the Table of Contents to navigate directly to that section.
- **Familiarize Yourself with Chapter Headings:** Each chapter addresses a specific aspect of Massachusetts driving regulations. Understand chapter headings to grasp the thematic organization. This enables the quick location of sections aligned with your learning objectives.

- **Pay Attention to Subheadings:** Within each chapter, subheadings further break down topics into specific areas. Whether it's traffic signs or safe driving practices, subheadings guide you to the exact information you seek. Scan through subheadings to pinpoint relevant content.
- **Use Index and Glossary:** The Index and Glossary are extremely useful tools for quick reference. If you encounter unfamiliar terms or need information on a specific topic, consult the Index. Similarly, the Glossary provides definitions, enhancing your understanding of key terminology used in the manual.
- **Embrace Visual Aids:** Strategic visual aids, like diagrams and illustrations, are placed throughout the manual. These visuals reinforce textual information, making complex concepts more accessible. Pay

attention to accompanying visuals for enhanced comprehension.

- **Interactive Elements:** Take advantage of interactive elements such as practice questions and scenarios. These not only reinforce learning but also serve as checkpoints to measure your understanding. Engaging with interactive features enhances the retention and application of knowledge.
- **Create Personal Notes or Highlights:** Make the manual your own by creating personal notes or highlights. If there's a specific rule or concept you find noteworthy, jot it down in the margins or use highlighting tools. This personalized touch serves as a quick reference during your study sessions.

Incorporating these navigation strategies transforms the manual into a user-friendly guide aligned with your learning preferences. Efficient navigation enhances your overall learning experience, ensuring you extract the maximum value from the Massachusetts Driver's Manual. Enjoy your exploration of the road to informed driving!

CHAPTER 2: THE LICENSING PROCESS

Welcome to Chapter 2, where we dive into the detailed intricacies of the licensing process in Massachusetts. Whether you're an eager new driver ready to hit the road or someone looking for a comprehensive understanding of the licensing journey, this chapter serves as your informative guide to the various license types, eligibility requirements, and application procedures.

Types of Licenses

Understanding the various types of licenses available in Massachusetts is a pivotal step in shaping your driving experience. This section provides a comprehensive exploration of various license types and their specific purposes, empowering you to choose the one that aligns perfectly with your needs.

- **Learner's Permit:** Tailored for new drivers, the learner's permit marks the beginning of your journey toward obtaining a full driver's license. It serves as your practice stage, allowing you to refine your driving skills under supervision before advancing to the next level.
- **Junior Operator License:** Targeted at drivers aged 16 ½ to 18, the Junior Operator License represents the next milestone. It introduces certain restrictions, such as limitations on passengers and nighttime driving. These restrictions gradually ease new drivers into the responsibilities of the road.
- **Full Operator License:** The coveted Full Operator License is the unrestricted license that most drivers aspire to achieve. It liberates you from the constraints associated with learner's permits or junior operator

licenses, providing the freedom to enjoy full driving privileges.

- **Motorcycle License:** Crafted for enthusiasts of two-wheeled travel, the Motorcycle License permits you to operate motorcycles, mopeds, and scooters on Massachusetts roads. It involves a unique set of skills and regulations tailored to the world of motorcycling.

- **Commercial Driver's License (CDL):** For those aspiring to operate commercial vehicles such as trucks or buses, the Commercial Driver's License (CDL) is essential. This license comes with additional endorsements and restrictions, ensuring that drivers are well-prepared to handle the distinct challenges of commercial driving.

- **Real ID:** In adherence to federal regulations, Massachusetts provides the Real ID, serving as a federally accepted form of identification. While not exclusive to driving, possessing a

Real ID driver's license ensures compliance with enhanced security standards for various purposes, including air travel.

Understanding the purpose of each license type is crucial for making informed decisions about your driving journey. Whether you're a novice driver exploring the roads for the first time or someone seeking additional driving privileges, this comprehensive overview serves as your guide to the diverse landscape of licenses available in Massachusetts. Choose wisely, and may your driving experiences be both safe and fulfilling!

Eligibility Requirements

Before you embark on the journey of obtaining your Massachusetts driver's license, understanding the eligibility requirements is crucial. This section delves into the criteria and qualifications necessary for application, ensuring you're well-prepared for the licensing process.

Age Requirements: The age criteria for applying for a driver's license in Massachusetts vary based on the type of license. Individuals can apply for a learner's permit at the age of 16. For junior operator licenses and full operator licenses, there are specific age-related eligibility criteria.

Age Check: The eligibility for legal driving in Massachusetts varies with age. Here's a breakdown:

- **16 Years Old:** Time to acquire your learner's permit and begin practice sessions with a licensed driver accompanying you. The learner's permit is a crucial step in learning the ropes of driving and understanding the rules of the road.
- **17 Years Old:** Spread your wings a bit with a junior operator's license. While enjoying more independence, be mindful of curfew and passenger restrictions. Daytime solo driving becomes an option, allowing you to gain valuable experience on the road.

- **18 Years Old:** Congratulations! You've reached the grand prize – the standard driver's license. At 18, freedom is now at your fingertips. However, it is important to remember that with tremendous power comes great responsibility. Obtaining your standard driver's license signifies a new level of independence and the responsibility to prioritize safety on the road.
- **Learner's Permit Eligibility:** To obtain a learner's permit, individuals must meet certain criteria, including completing a comprehensive driver's education program that includes both classroom instruction and behind-the-wheel training. This ensures that new drivers acquire essential knowledge and skills for safe driving.
- **Junior Operator License Requirements:** The transition to a junior operator license involves fulfilling additional requirements, such as completing a specified number of

supervised driving hours and holding a learner's permit for a designated period. These requirements are designed to provide new drivers with practical experience before advancing to a higher license level.

- **Full Operator License Qualifications:** Achieving a full operator license typically requires maintaining a junior operator license without incidents for a specified duration. Depending on age and driving history, additional training or criteria may be applicable.

- **Commercial Driver's License (CDL) Eligibility:** Individuals aspiring to obtain a Commercial Driver's License (CDL) must meet specific eligibility criteria, which may include age restrictions, completion of a CDL training program, and successful performance in relevant tests to demonstrate knowledge and skills.

- **Real ID Requirements:** For a Real ID driver's license, applicants are required to submit additional documentation to establish identity and residency. This enhanced form of identification is crucial for compliance with federal regulations, extending beyond its use for driving purposes.

Whether you're acquiring your learner's permit, junior operator's license, or standard driver's license, each stage comes with its own set of rules and privileges. Make the most of this journey, stay informed about driving regulations, and embrace the responsibility that comes with being a licensed driver.

- **Residency Matters:** To declare the open road as your kingdom, it's imperative to be a legal resident of Massachusetts. Demonstrating your commitment to the driving adventures involves providing proof, such as a utility bill or lease agreement. This documentation not only establishes your residency but also ensures that you're ready to embrace the responsibilities and privileges that come with navigating the roads of Massachusetts.

- **Vision Quests:** Maintaining clear eyesight is crucial for safe driving. As you journey toward obtaining your driver's license, be ready to undergo a vision test at the RMV. If glasses or lenses enhance your vision, consider them your trusty driving shield, ensuring you navigate the roads with optimal clarity.
- **Knowledge is Power:** Traffic laws go beyond being mere facts; they represent the code of the road. Demonstrate your understanding by undertaking a written knowledge test. Think of it as your superhero training montage, equipping you with the knowledge to confidently conquer the streets with a blend of safety and savvy.

Bonus Round: Beyond the Basics:
- **Social Security Number:** Your driving superhero alias.
- **Medical Checks:** Certain medical conditions might need restrictions or special licenses. The RMV provides resources and guidance to ensure everyone drives safely.
- **Proof of Identity:** Whether it's a passport or a driver's license from another state, show the RMV who you are!

Application Procedures

Embarking on the journey to obtain your Massachusetts driver's license involves a series of steps and procedures. Follow this step-by-step walkthrough to navigate the application process seamlessly and ensure a smooth transition from a learner's permit to a licensed driver.

Step 1: Gather Your Gear:

- **Proof of Identity:** Passport, driver's license from another state, or birth certificate – show the RMV who you are!
- **Proof of Residency:** Utility bill, lease agreement, or bank statement – prove you're a Massachusetts resident ready to conquer the local roads.
- **Social Security Number:** This helps the RMV identify you, like your driving superhero alias.
- **Medical Information:** If necessary, bring documentation of any medical conditions that might affect your driving.
- **Knowledge Arsenal:** Brush up on your traffic laws – the written knowledge test is your first hurdle!

Step 2: Head to the RMV Headquarters:

- **Locate your nearest RMV branch:** No need to travel far, find a convenient spot to start your adventure.

- **Make an appointment online:** Skip the line and schedule a specific time to avoid waiting in the hero HQ.
- **Gear up with the right forms:** Download or pick up the application forms in advance, fill them out neatly (no villainous scribbles!), and bring them with you.

Step 3: Navigate the RMV Labyrinth:
- **Check-in with the friendly RMV staff:** They're not your enemies, they're here to guide you through the process.
- **Prepare for your photo op:** Smile for the camera, it'll be your driving companion for years to come.
- **Ace the written knowledge test:** Unleash your inner traffic law superhero! Remember, practice makes perfect.

Obtain a Learner's Permit:
- Attend a Massachusetts-approved driver's education program.

- Complete the required classroom instruction and behind-the-wheel training.
- Pass a written learner's permit exam at the RMV.

Practice with Your Learner's Permit:

- Hold your learner's permit for the required practice period.
- Accumulate the mandated supervised driving hours with a qualified sponsor.

Schedule and Complete a Road Test:

- Schedule a road test appointment with the RMV.
- Successfully pass the road test, demonstrating your driving skills.

Upgrade to a Junior Operator License:

- With a successful road test, upgrade from the learner's permit to a junior operator license.
- Adhere to any restrictions associated with the junior operator license, such as limitations on passengers and nighttime driving.

Fulfill Additional Requirements for Full Operator License:
- Hold the junior operator license for the required period without incidents.
- Complete any additional training or requirements based on your age and driving history.

Apply for a Full Operator License:
- Submit an application for a full operator license at the RMV.
- Pay the applicable fees for the license.

Commercial Driver's License (CDL) Application:
- If pursuing a CDL, meet the age and training requirements.
- Pass the written CDL knowledge tests for the specific class and endorsements needed.
- Schedule and complete the CDL road skills test.

Real ID Application (Optional):
- If opting for a Real ID, present additional documentation to establish identity and residency.
- Ensure compliance with federal requirements for enhanced security.

Renew Your License:
- Regularly renew your Massachusetts driver's license to ensure its validity.

Stay Informed:
- Keep abreast of any changes in Massachusetts driving regulations.
- Stay informed about license renewal dates and any additional requirements.

Bonus Round: Remember the Rules:
- The application process might vary slightly depending on your specific circumstances. Check the RMV website for the latest updates and specific requirements.

- **Fees apply:** Be prepared to pay for your permit, license, and any additional tests or services.
- **Patience is a virtue:** The process might take some time, so don't get discouraged. Stay focused, keep practicing, and your driving dreams will soon become a reality.

By following these steps, you'll navigate the application process with confidence, ensuring that you meet the necessary criteria and adhere to the specific procedures for each stage of your journey. May your path to obtaining a Massachusetts driver's license be smooth and filled with success. Safe travels on your road to licensed driving!

Learner's Permit Restrictions

Congratulations on obtaining your learner's permit in Massachusetts! As you begin your journey toward a driver's license, it's vital to comprehend the restrictions and regulations that accompany this initial phase. Let's explore the training grounds and delve into the limitations of your learner's permit, adding valuable insights along the way:

- **Supervised Driving Only:** Your learner's permit grants you the privilege of driving, but only under supervision. You can operate a vehicle when accompanied by a licensed adult aged at least 21, with a minimum of one year of driving experience.
- **Valuable Insight:** Use this period to glean practical knowledge from experienced drivers. Take advantage of the opportunity to ask questions, seek guidance, and build a solid foundation for your driving skills.
- **Passenger Restrictions:** Passenger restrictions come into play during the learner's permit phase. You're permitted to transport only immediate family members unless supervised by a licensed driving instructor.
- **Valuable Insight:** Focus on honing your driving skills with family members as

passengers. Their familiarity can create a supportive environment, aiding in your learning process.

- **No Nighttime Driving Without Supervision:** Nighttime driving, defined as 30 minutes after sunset to 30 minutes before sunrise, is prohibited unless supervised by a licensed parent, guardian, or an individual aged at least 21 with a minimum of one year of driving experience.
- **Valuable Insight:** Respect nighttime driving restrictions as they ensure you gain experience under safer conditions. Utilize this time to focus on developing your daytime driving skills.
- **Hands-Free Device Required:** Driving with a learner's permit mandates the use of a hands-free device for any electronic communication or entertainment devices.
- **Valuable Insight:** Cultivate good habits early on, such as using hands-free devices.

This not only ensures compliance but also emphasizes the importance of minimizing distractions while driving.

- **Compliance with Traffic Laws:** Strict adherence to all traffic laws and regulations is imperative. Non-compliance may result in penalties that could impact your progression to the next stage of licensing.
- **Valuable Insight:** Treat every traffic law as a lesson. Understanding and following regulations contribute to your overall safety and prepare you for responsible driving in the future.
- **No Towing:** Learner's permit holders are not allowed to tow other vehicles.
- **Valuable Insight:** Concentrate on mastering the basics of driving without additional complexities. Towing involves advanced skills; your learner's permit phase is about building a strong foundation.

Understanding and respecting these restrictions is not only crucial for your safety but also for the safety of others on the road. The learner's permit phase offers valuable supervised practice, allowing you to gradually build your skills and confidence. As you navigate the training grounds, consider each rule as a stepping stone toward your goal of becoming a responsible and skilled driver. Safe travels on the road to licensed driving!

CHAPTER 3: RULES OF THE ROAD

Welcome to Chapter 3, where we delve into the foundational rules and regulations that govern the roadways of Massachusetts. Whether you're a new driver eager to grasp the essentials or a seasoned driver seeking a refresher, this chapter serves as your guide to understanding and navigating the intricate network of rules ensuring safe and harmonious travel.

Traffic Signs and Signals

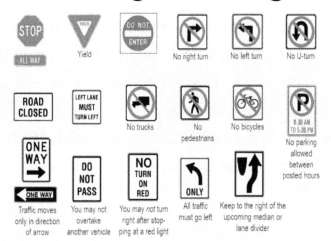

In the dynamic world of driving, communication is paramount. Traffic signs and signals serve as the language of the road, conveying crucial information to drivers. In this section, we'll delve into the meanings and implications of various traffic signs and signals, empowering you to navigate Massachusetts roadways with confidence and precision.

Regulatory Signs:

- **Stop Sign:** An octagonal red warrior demanding a complete stop at intersections. Come to a full stop, yield to cross traffic – no rolling through!
- **Yield Sign:** A triangular friend suggesting courtesy. Slow down and prepare to stop if necessary to yield the right of way to others. Sharing the road is key!
- **Do Not Enter Sign (Square with White Bar):** Prohibits entry to a restricted area.

- **Speed Limit Sign:** A circular number setting the pace. Obey the posted speed limit to avoid speeding tickets.
- **One-Way Signs:** Arrows pointing the way. Follow the indicated directions to avoid confusion.
- **No Parking Signs:** Red circles with white lines indicating parking prohibition. Find a legal spot to avoid tickets and unhappy neighbors.

Warning Signs:
- **Curve Ahead Sign:** Alerts drivers to an upcoming curve in the road.
- **School Zone Sign:** Indicates the presence of a school zone, requiring reduced speed.
- **Traffic Signal Ahead Sign:** Warns of an upcoming traffic signal.

Guide Signs:
- **Route Marker Signs:** Display the route number and guide drivers along specific highways.

- **Exit Signs:** Indicate upcoming exits on highways.
- **Destination Signs:** Provide information about locations and distances to various destinations.

Construction and Maintenance Signs:
- **Road Work Ahead Sign:** Warns of construction or maintenance activities ahead.
- **Detour Sign:** Redirects drivers along an alternative route due to road closures.

Traffic Signals:
- **Red Light:** Demands a complete halt. Stop and wait for the green light to resume your journey.
- **Yellow Light:** Signals caution. If safely within the intersection, proceed with caution; otherwise, prepare to stop.
- **Green Light:** Grants the right of way. Proceed steadily but stay alert for pedestrians and other vehicles.

Bonus Round: Remember These Gems:
- Different traffic lights have unique features like turning arrows or pedestrian signals. Pay attention to the details!
- Regulatory signs convey diverse information. Be a sign detective and read them all!
- Warning signs act as caution flags, alerting you to upcoming hazards. Slow down and adjust your driving accordingly.
- Construction zones require extra caution. Follow the orange cone maze and respect the workers building a better road.

Understanding these signs and signals is crucial for safe and efficient navigation. They provide guidance, warnings, and regulations contributing to the overall order and safety of the road. As you encounter these visual cues on your driving journey, interpret them with confidence, knowing that you're fluent in the language of the road. Safe travels!

Right of Way

In the intricate dance of traffic, the concept of right-of-way is a guiding principle that ensures smooth and safe interactions between drivers. Understanding and respecting the right-of-way contributes to the harmony of the road. In this section, let's explore the principles of right-of-way to empower you with the knowledge to navigate traffic safely.

At Intersections:

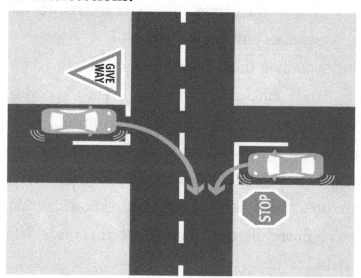

- **Uncontrolled Intersections:** The vehicle that arrives first or the one on the right generally has the right-of-way at intersections without traffic signals or signs.
- **Four-Way Stops:** The first vehicle to come to a complete stop at the intersection is typically the first to proceed.

Turning Right or Left:

- **Turning Right:** When turning right at an intersection with a green light or stop sign, you usually have the right-of-way, but be cautious of pedestrians and oncoming traffic.

- **Turning Left:** When turning left, yield to oncoming traffic. If there's a green arrow or dedicated left-turn lane, you have the right-of-way.

Pedestrians and Crosswalks:
- **Crosswalks:** Pedestrians are granted the right-of-way at crosswalks. Drivers should yield to pedestrians crossing the road.
- **Pedestrian Signals:** Obey pedestrian signals at traffic lights. When the "Walk" signal is visible, pedestrians are granted the right of way.

Emergency Vehicles:
- **Sirens and Lights:** Vehicles with emergency sirens and flashing lights always have the right-of-way. Move to the right to provide a space for them to pass comfortably.

Yielding in Traffic Flow:
- **Highways and On-Ramps:** When entering a highway or merging onto an on-ramp, yield to vehicles already on the main road.

- **Rotaries and Roundabouts:** Give the right-of-way to vehicles already in the rotary or roundabout. Before you enter, wait for a safe opening.

Bonus Round: Pro Tips for the Right-of-Way Dance:

- **Communicate Clearly:** Use your turn signals to let other drivers know your intentions. Remember, they're not mind readers!
- **Additional Tip:** Make eye contact with other drivers, enhancing communication.
- **Don't Be Aggressive:** Don't force your way through traffic or try to bully other drivers. Patience and courtesy are key to a smooth flow.
- **Additional Tip:** Allow extra time for unexpected delays, reducing stress for you and others.
- **Stay Alert:** Be aware of your surroundings and anticipate what other drivers might do.

Remember, defensive driving is the best kind of driving!

- **Additional Tip:** Minimize distractions like phones, focusing on the road for a safer drive.
- **Know the Exceptions:** There are some exceptions to the right-of-way rules, such as emergency vehicles and certain intersections with specific signage. Familiarize yourself with the local traffic laws to avoid surprises.
- **Additional Tip:** Attend local traffic safety seminars or workshops for updated knowledge.

Understanding the right-of-way enhances your ability to anticipate and react to traffic situations. It promotes courteous and safe driving practices, contributing to a smoother flow of traffic. As you navigate the roads, remember that right-of-way is not just a rule; it's a principle of mutual respect that ensures everyone's journey is safer and more efficient. Safe travels!

Speed Limits

The speed at which you travel on Massachusetts roadways is a crucial element of road safety and compliance with traffic regulations. Let's explore the established speed limits in Massachusetts and understand the significance of adhering to these guidelines.

- **Residential Areas:** In residential areas, where homes and pedestrian activity are prevalent, the speed limit is typically set lower, ranging from 20 to 30 miles per hour to ensure the safety of residents and road users.
- **School Zones:** Near schools, speed limits are significantly reduced, often ranging from 20 to 25 miles per hour to prioritize the safety of children. Be extra cautious during designated school hours and adhere to posted speed limits.
- **Urban Areas:** Within urban areas and city streets, speed limits vary but are generally

lower than on highways. Common speed limits in urban zones range from 25 to 35 miles per hour, ensuring safe navigation through traffic and intersections.

- **Rural Roads:** On rural roads, where traffic is less congested, speed limits may be higher, ranging from 35 to 55 miles per hour, depending on factors such as road design and traffic density.
- **Highways:** Highways and expressways in Massachusetts are designed to facilitate smoother traffic flow, often featuring elevated speed limits. Speed limits on these roadways typically vary between 55 to 65 miles per hour, with specific limits clearly indicated on road signs.
- **Interstate Highways:** When it comes to Interstate Highways, the thrill of multi-lane expressways invites drivers to feel the rush, but responsibility is key. The established legal speed limit is a comfortable 65 mph,

emphasizing the importance of cruising in the fast lane with a safety-first mindset, except on specific stretches where alternative limits are posted.

- **Divided Highways:** For Divided Highways, offering a seamless journey beyond the Interstate, a steady pace is encouraged. The usual posted limit is set at 50 mph, reinforcing the need for a balanced and secure driving experience even without the presence of stop signs and traffic lights.

- **Undivided Highways:** Undivided Highways, where caution is paramount due to two-way traffic, prompt a further reduction in speed limits to 40 mph. This adjustment ensures that drivers have ample time to respond to oncoming vehicles and unexpected situations, promoting a heightened level of awareness on these road segments.

Significance of Adhering to Speed Limits:

- **Safety:** Following speed limits enhances safety by providing drivers with sufficient time to react to changing road conditions and potential hazards.
- **Traffic Flow:** Consistent adherence to speed limits contributes to a smoother flow of traffic, reducing the likelihood of congestion and accidents.
- **Legal Compliance:** Adhering to posted speed limits ensures legal compliance, avoiding penalties such as fines and points on your driving record.

Bonus Round: Remember These Tempo Twists:

- **School Zones:** Exercise extra vigilance and slow down to 20 mph in designated school zones to protect our tiniest road users when school is in session.
- **Construction Zones:** Be cautious around orange cones and flashing lights, signaling reduced speeds in construction zones—often

as low as 35 mph—to ensure everyone's safety.

- **Weather Warnings:** Adjust your speed according to weather conditions. In rain, snow, or fog, lower visibility demands a slower rhythm, even below the posted limit, to navigate safely.

Understanding and respecting speed limits is not just a legal obligation; it's a commitment to creating a safer and more efficient driving environment for all road users. As you traverse the Bay State's roads, let the posted speed limits be your guide to a responsible and secure driving experience. Safe travels!

Lane Usage and Changes

Mastering the intricacies of lane usage and changes is crucial for a seamless and safe traffic flow on Massachusetts roads. This section provides insights into proper lane procedures, ensuring responsible driving.

- **Lane Discipline:** Follow proper lane discipline, staying within your designated lane. Avoid unnecessary weaving, promoting consistent and predictable lane usage for overall traffic safety.
- **Right Lane Travel:** The right lane is generally designated for slower-moving traffic and serves as the default lane for drivers, except when passing or getting ready for a right turn. Utilize the right lane if you are driving at a slower pace than the overall flow of traffic.
- **Left Lane (Passing Lane):** Known as the passing lane, use the left lane for overtaking slower vehicles or when driving at a faster pace than the traffic in the right lanes. Return to the right lane after passing to maintain smooth traffic flow.
- **Double Lines are Impassable Walls:** Solid white lines between lanes are strict boundaries, allowing lane changes only in

emergencies. Respect these borders to avoid issues with law enforcement.
- **Center and Multiple Lanes:** On roads with multiple lanes, use center lanes for general travel. Avoid lingering in left lanes if not actively passing other vehicles.

Lane Changes: Changing lanes is a cooperative dance:
- **Signal Your Intentions:** Indicate your intention to change lanes by using your turn signal. Check your mirrors, look over your shoulder to check blind spots and ensure sufficient space for a safe merge.
- **Timing is Everything:** Signal well in advance, at least 3 seconds, to alert fellow drivers. This courteous gesture minimizes surprises.
- **Check Blind Spots:** Turn your head and check blind spots before changing lanes. This precaution prevents unwanted surprises on the road.

- **No Cutting Off:** Patience is key; wait for a comfortable opening to avoid aggressive maneuvers that lead to honks and potential issues with law enforcement.
- **Multi-Lane Mayhem:** Change lanes gradually, one at a time, signaling and checking blind spots for each move. Smooth transitions enhance safety and traffic flow.
- **Yield to Emergency Vehicles:** When emergency vehicles approach, yield by moving to the right, providing a clear path for their swift passage.
- **Construction Zones:** Follow lane markings and signs in construction zones. Be attentive to temporary lane shifts and reduced speeds for the safety of drivers and workers.
  - **Highway Exits and Entrances:** Plan for highway exits, using appropriate lanes to merge or exit. Avoid

last-minute changes to enhance traffic flow.

Bonus Round: Mastering the Lane Maze:
- **Merge Lanes Smoothly:** Enter highways with finesse, matching traffic speed and avoiding forceful maneuvers.
- **Yield to Emergency Vehicles:** Promptly pull over for emergency vehicles, letting them pass swiftly in urgent situations.
- **Construction Zones:** Pay attention to signs and flaggers in construction zones, adjust speed, and practice patience.

Understanding and applying these lane guidelines enhances overall safety and efficiency on Massachusetts roads. Developing good lane habits contributes to a cooperative and secure driving environment. Safe travels on the Bay State's pathways!

CHAPTER 4: SAFE DRIVING PRACTICES

Welcome to Chapter 4, where we explore crucial safe driving practices essential for a responsible and secure driving experience on Massachusetts roads. Whether you're a novice building a strong foundation or a seasoned driver seeking a refresher, this chapter guides you in mastering techniques that contribute to a safer driving environment.

Defensive Driving Techniques

Defensive driving is more than a skill; it's a mindset empowering you to navigate roads with heightened awareness, anticipate hazards, and make informed decisions for your safety and others. In this section, we delve into key defensive driving techniques to elevate your safety on Massachusetts roads.

- **Stay Vigilant and Aware:** Maintain continuous awareness by scanning the road, checking mirrors, and staying attuned to other drivers. Be alert to potential hazards, including unexpected movements from pedestrians and cyclists.

- **Keep a Safe Following Distance:** Adhere to the three-second rule for a safe following distance. Increase this distance in adverse weather conditions or when driving at higher speeds. Maintaining space provides time to react to sudden changes.
- **Anticipate Potential Hazards:** Scan for upcoming intersections, pedestrian crossings, and changes in traffic patterns to anticipate potential hazards. Proactive decisions and prompt reactions to unexpected situations are crucial.
- **Use Your Mirrors Effectively:** Enhance situational awareness by effectively using rearview mirrors, and side mirrors, and checking blind spots before changing lanes or making turns.

- **Be Mindful of Speed Limits:** Adhere to speed limits and adjust based on road conditions for better control and safer reactions.
- **Avoid Distractions:** Minimize distractions like phone use or adjusting the radio to stay focused on the road, enabling better responses to changing conditions.
- **Prepare for the Unexpected:** Anticipate unexpected actions from other drivers, such as sudden lane changes or stops. A proactive mindset ensures readiness for the unexpected.
- **Use Your Turn Signals:** Signal intentions well in advance for changing lanes, turning, or merging. Think of it as a polite way of saying, "Excuse me, I'm planning to move over here!"
- **Mind Your Headlights:** Don't blind oncoming drivers! Use low beams in low-light conditions and high beams

cautiously. Courtesy in lighting ensures a smoother journey for everyone.
- **Honk Strategically:** Use your horn sparingly for emergencies or warnings, avoiding unnecessary noise.

Bonus Round: Remember These Defensive Gems:
- **Practice makes perfect:** Regularly practice defensive driving techniques for confidence behind the wheel.
- **Stay calm and collected:** Avoid road rage; keep calm, breathe, and refrain from aggressive behavior.
- **Be prepared for the unexpected:** Keep an emergency kit, stay aware, and adjust driving in unforeseen situations.

Embrace these defensive driving techniques to become a confident and capable driver, contributing to responsible road use and making Massachusetts roads safer. Safe travels as you implement these techniques on your driving journey!

Handling Intersections

Intersections, where diverse vehicle paths converge, demand quick, informed decisions from drivers. This section offers guidance on mastering the art of navigating intersections safely and efficiently on Massachusetts roads.

- **Observe Right-of-Way Rules:** Comprehend and adhere to right-of-way rules. At uncontrolled intersections, yield to the first arriving vehicle or the one on the right. Respect traffic signals and signs, maintaining the established order of movement.
- **Approach with Caution:** Exercise caution at intersections, particularly when visibility is limited. Reduce speed and be ready to yield when needed. A cautious approach

heightens your responsiveness to unforeseen situations.

- **Check for Pedestrians and Bicyclists:** Prioritize the safety of pedestrians and bicyclists. Scrutinize crosswalks and designated bike lanes before proceeding through intersections. In crosswalks, yield the right-of-way to pedestrians.

- **Signal Your Intentions:** Utilize turn signals to communicate your plans to fellow road users. Clearly indicate whether you intend to turn left, right, or proceed straight, promoting smoother traffic flow and reducing confusion.

- **Be Aware of Multiple Lanes:** In intersections with multiple lanes, select the appropriate lane for your intended direction. Ensure you're in the correct lane well before reaching the intersection to avoid last-minute maneuvers.

- **Avoid Blocking Intersections:** Refrain from entering an intersection if traffic conditions suggest getting stuck when the light changes. Blocking intersections disrupts traffic flow and may lead to gridlock.
- **Observe Traffic Lights and Signs:** Pay close attention to traffic lights and signs governing the intersection. Red signifies stop, green signals go, and yellow indicates caution. Adhere to designated lanes per posted signs.
- **Watch for Turning Vehicles:** Exercise caution when vehicles turn left across your path or make a right turn from the opposite direction. Anticipate turning vehicle movements and be ready to yield if necessary.

Bonus Round: Intersections Come in Different Flavors:
- **Roundabouts:** Treat them like traffic circles. Yield to vehicles in the roundabout, then enter and proceed counter-clockwise.

Patience is key, and avoid getting caught in a roundabout waltz!

- **Merging Lanes:** Adjust speed, signal intentions, and check blind spots before merging smoothly into traffic.
- **School Zones and Crosswalks:** Slow down, exercise extra caution, and yield to pedestrians. Future pedestrians deserve our utmost respect and attention.

Mastering intersection navigation is crucial for safe and efficient driving. By adopting these practices, you not only enhance your safety, but you also contribute to the overall flow and orderliness of traffic. As you encounter intersections on your Massachusetts journeys, may your approach be measured, and your decisions well-informed. Safe travels!

Sharing the Road with Pedestrians and Bicyclists

Navigating Massachusetts roads involves more than just interacting with fellow motorists; it also requires keen awareness and consideration for pedestrians and bicyclists who share the same spaces. Let's explore best practices for sharing the road harmoniously and ensuring the safety of all road users.

Pedestrians: Our Footloose Friends on the Road:

- **Yield to Pedestrians:** Pedestrians have right of way in crosswalks and intersections. Always yield to pedestrians, regardless of whether the crosswalk is marked or unmarked. Be cautious, especially when there are a lot of pedestrians around.

- **Be Aware of Crosswalks:** Approach marked and unmarked crosswalks with caution. Slow down and be ready to stop so that pedestrians can cross safely. Check your blind spots for any approaching pedestrians.

- **Look Out, They're Everywhere!:** Pedestrians can emerge unexpectedly from various corners, particularly near bus stops and crosswalks. Stay vigilant, scan the surroundings ahead, and anticipate their movements. Remember, they're not invisible ninjas!
- **Honking Isn't the Harmony We Need:** Exercise patience and refrain from unnecessary horn usage. Abrupt horn blasts can startle pedestrians and create confusion. Keep in mind that courtesy is the soundtrack to maintaining a smooth traffic flow.

Cyclists: Two-Wheeled Wonders Sharing the Asphalt:

- **Give Bicyclists Adequate Space:** When sharing the road with bicyclists, provide ample space for their safety. Leave at least three feet of space when passing a bicyclist and avoid crowding them. Patience is key when waiting to pass safely.

- **Watch for Bicyclists in Bike Lanes:** Respect designated bike lanes. Check for bicyclists before turning across a bike lane and be cautious when merging or crossing bike lanes. Bicyclists have the right to use these lanes safely.

- **Doors Can Be Dangerous Traps:** Prioritize safety by checking your mirrors and blind spots before opening your car door. Cyclists can easily get caught in the swing, leading to potentially serious accidents. Remember, their safety is literally in your hands!

- **Exercise Caution at Intersections:** Be particularly cautious at intersections where interactions between motorists, pedestrians, and bicyclists are common. Pay attention to traffic signals and signs, and yield the right-of-way as appropriate.

- **Use Turn Signals:** Communicate your intentions by using turn signals when turning or changing lanes. This allows pedestrians and bicyclists to anticipate your movements and act accordingly.
- **Avoid Distractions:** Minimize distractions, such as using your phone or adjusting the radio, to ensure you are fully aware of your surroundings. Distraction-free driving is crucial when sharing the road with vulnerable users.
- **Exercise Patience:** Exercise patience and understanding when sharing the road. Bicyclists may travel at different speeds, and pedestrians may have varied levels of mobility. Approach interactions with a mindset of shared responsibility.

Bonus Round: Harmony Tips for All Road Users:

- **Distractions are the Discordant Notes:** Avoid discord on the road by putting your phone down! Eating, texting, or adjusting the radio can cause you to miss crucial cues from pedestrians and cyclists. Stay focused on the road, keep your mind sharp, and remember, the world can wait until you reach your destination.

- **Predictability is the Sweetest Melody:** Create a harmonious driving experience by signaling your intentions clearly, obeying traffic rules, and avoiding erratic maneuvers. Predictability makes the road safer and more enjoyable for everyone.
- **Patience is the Key to the Perfect Tempo:** Don't become a road rage maestro! Maintain a steady tempo in congested areas, yield when necessary, and remember, courtesy and patience contribute to a smoother and more harmonious traffic flow.

By embracing these practices, you play a vital role in fostering a culture of safety, respect, and shared responsibility on Massachusetts roads. Every interaction with pedestrians and cyclists is an opportunity to create a positive and secure environment for all road users. As you navigate diverse road scenarios, let your actions reflect a commitment to harmonious and considerate road sharing. Safe travels!

Adverse Weather Conditions

In Massachusetts, where weather patterns can be diverse and dynamic, being prepared for adverse weather conditions is a crucial aspect of safe driving. This section equips you with the knowledge and strategies to navigate through rain, snow, and other challenging weather scenarios with confidence.

- **Rainy Weather:** When driving in the rain, reduce your speed as wet roads can be slippery. Increase the following distance to allow for safe braking. Ensure your headlights are on for better visibility, and use windshield wipers to maintain a clear view.

- **Snow and Ice:** In snowy or icy conditions, slow down and drive with extra caution. Equip your vehicle with snow tires if necessary and maintain a safe distance from other vehicles. Use anti-lock brakes (ABS) if available and avoid sudden movements.
- **Foggy Conditions:** In foggy weather, reduce your speed and use low-beam headlights to improve visibility. Refrain from utilizing high beams, as they may cause reflection in fog, diminishing visibility. Be attentive to road markings and signs.
- **Strong Winds:** Exercise caution in windy conditions, especially on exposed roads or bridges. Keep a firm grip on the steering wheel, and be prepared for sudden gusts. Maintain a safe distance from larger vehicles, as they can be affected by crosswinds.
- **Hailstorms:** If you find yourself caught in a hailstorm, prioritize safety by locating a

secure place to pull over, such as a parking lot or rest area. Shield your vehicle by parking under a structure if one is available. For personal safety, remain inside the vehicle to avoid potential injuries caused by hail.

- **Thunderstorms:** In the midst of thunderstorms, it's crucial to adapt your driving behavior. Slow down, switch on your headlights if visibility is compromised, and steer clear of flooded areas, where water levels can escalate rapidly. If visibility is severely impacted, consider finding a safe spot to pull over.
- **Hot Weather:** As temperatures rise, take a moment to ensure your vehicle is adequately cooled before hitting the road. Stay hydrated, keep water on hand, and be mindful of the impact of hot pavement on tire performance.
- **Check Weather Forecasts:** Empower yourself with weather knowledge by staying updated on forecasts and road conditions

before embarking on your journey. Informed decisions about your route and driving conditions can make a significant difference.

- **Plan for Extra Travel Time:** In challenging weather conditions, it's wise to plan for additional travel time to ensure a safe and unrushed journey. Factor in potential delays, and communicate your expected arrival time to others.

Bonus Round: Weather Warriors Wisdom:

- **Plan Your Trip Wisely:** Before setting out, check the weather forecast and consider postponing your trip if severe conditions are predicted. Remember, sometimes the safest choice is to stay put.

- **Keep an Emergency Kit Handy:** Prepare for unforeseen circumstances by packing essentials like blankets, water, non-perishable food, a flashlight, and a first-aid kit. You never know when these items might come in handy during bad weather.

- **Stay Alert and Focused:** Eliminate distractions like phone use or eating. Stay focused on the road, and be vigilant for changes in weather conditions. A concentrated mind is better equipped to navigate through storms.

By integrating these tactics into your driving strategy, you can confidently confront adverse weather conditions. Preparedness and cautious driving not only ensure your safety but also contribute to a secure road environment for everyone. As you face the diverse weather challenges on Massachusetts roads, may your journey be marked by safety and secure travels.

CHAPTER 5: VEHICLE OPERATION

Welcome to Chapter 5, where we delve into the intricacies of operating a vehicle in the Bay State. A pivotal element of vehicle operation lies in comprehending the diverse controls and instruments that form your driving cockpit. In this section, we'll introduce you to these indispensable elements, empowering you to navigate Massachusetts roads with assurance.

Vehicle Controls and Instruments

Vehicle Control

- **Steering Wheel:** The steering wheel serves as your primary tool for steering your vehicle. Maintain a comfortable grip and execute controlled, smooth movements.
- **Accelerator (Gas Pedal):** The accelerator dictates your vehicle's speed. Apply gentle

pressure for smooth acceleration and release it gradually for deceleration.

- **Brake Pedal:** Essential for slowing down or stopping your vehicle, the brake pedal requires consistent pressure for effective braking.
- **Clutch (Manual Transmission):** In vehicles with manual transmission, the clutch pedal disengages the engine from the transmission during gear shifts.
- **Gear Shift (Manual Transmission):** Exclusive to manual transmission vehicles, the gear shift allows you to select different gears. Practice seamless transitions for optimal performance.
- **Parking Brake:** Also referred to as the handbrake, the parking brake is crucial for securing your vehicle when parked. Engage it fully to prevent unintended movement.

Vehicle Instruments:

- **Speedometer:** Keep an eye on the speedometer to stay within the designated speed limits and drive safely, measuring your vehicle's speed in miles per hour (mph).
- **Tachometer (Manual Transmission):** For manual transmission vehicles, the tachometer reveals the engine's revolutions per minute (RPM), aiding in optimizing gear shifts.
- **Fuel Gauge:** Monitor the fuel gauge to track the amount of fuel in your tank and prevent running out of gas during your journey.
- **Temperature Gauge:** The temperature gauge provides insights into the engine's temperature. Keep it within the typical range to avoid overheating.
- **Oil Pressure Gauge:** The oil pressure gauge oversees the engine's oil circulation. Low oil pressure may indicate issues, necessitating prompt attention.

- **Check Engine Light:** The check engine light serves as an alert for potential vehicle issues. Consult your vehicle's manual or a mechanic for diagnostic assistance.
- **Turn Signals:** Activate turn signals well in advance of turning or changing lanes to communicate your intentions to other drivers on the road.
- **Headlights and High Beams:** Familiarize yourself with headlight controls, using low beams in low-light conditions and high beams on unlit roads for enhanced visibility.

Bonus Round: Control Panel Gems:
- **Headlights and Wipers:** Adjust headlights and use wipers based on visibility conditions. Dim headlights for oncoming traffic, and activate wipers when it starts raining, prioritizing clear vision for safe driving.
- **Mirrors:** Regularly check your rearview window and side mirrors to stay aware of

your surroundings and optimize blind spot coverage.

- **Radio and Climate Control:** Enjoy your favorite tunes and maintain a comfortable temperature, but be cautious of distractions. Keep the volume at a reasonable level and make quick glances, not prolonged stares, while adjusting climate settings.

Mastering these vehicle controls and instruments is pivotal for safe and efficient driving in Massachusetts. As you become proficient in handling your vehicle, you not only enhance your overall driving experience but also contribute to road safety. Wishing you safe travels as you refine the art of vehicle operation in the Bay State!

Basic Vehicle Maintenance

Ensuring that your car runs smoothly is more than simply a matter of reliability; it is also about safety and durability. This section delves into key car maintenance procedures that will keep your ride functioning smoothly on Massachusetts' various routes.

- **Regular Oil Changes:** Schedule frequent oil changes to ensure optimal engine lubrication. Refer to your vehicle's manual for suggested intervals, and use the proper oil type.
- **Tire Care:** Check and maintain tire pressure at specified levels. Rotate tires at regular intervals to ensure equal wear. Check for damage or uneven tread.
- **Brake Inspection:** Check your brakes regularly for wear indications such as squeaks or grinds. Replace brake pads or shoes as needed to maintain proper braking system operation.
- **Fluid Levels:** Check fluid levels for coolant, gearbox, brake, and power steering. Fill up or change fluids according to your vehicle's maintenance plan.

- **Brake Fluid:** Check the amount and color of the brake fluid regularly to ensure efficient braking. Dark or hazy fluid may signal problems that need a mechanic's check. Remember that good brakes provide peace of mind!
- **Windshield Washer Fluid:** To maintain vision in rainstorms, keep your windshield washer fluid filled up, particularly throughout the winter. Clear sight is essential for safe driving!
- **Coolant Check:** To prevent engine overheating, check coolant levels regularly, particularly before lengthy excursions. Leaks or discoloration may indicate a problem, necessitating a mechanic's inspection. Cool engines are happy engines!
- **Battery Health:** Inspect the battery for corrosion and ensure secure connections. Make sure it's properly attached and replace

it according to your vehicle's manual instructions.

- **Air Filter Replacement:** Regularly replace the air filter for optimal engine performance and fuel economy. A blocked filter may reduce engine efficiency.
- **Wiper Blades:** Replace wiper blades that exhibit wear or streaking. Clear visibility, particularly during inclement weather, is essential.
- **Headlights and Taillights:** Regularly examine and clean headlights, taillights, and turn signals. To ensure maximum visibility and compliance with safety rules, change lights promptly.
- **Alignment and Suspension:** Maintain appropriate wheel alignment to minimize uneven tire wear. Check the suspension system for evidence of damage or wear, such as bouncing or swaying.

- **Check for Leaks:** Regularly check for leaks in oil, coolant, and brake fluid. Address any leaks as soon as possible to minimize further damage and maintain a safe driving experience.
- **Maintain a Service Schedule:** Follow the suggested service schedule in your vehicle's owner's manual. Regular expert inspections and maintenance help to ensure long-term reliability.

Bonus Round: Maintenance Tips:
- **Regular Inspections:** Schedule regular inspections with your technician. Early diagnosis of possible difficulties may help you save time and money.
- **Listen to Your Car:** Pay attention to any strange sounds or changes in performance. Early diagnosis is critical to avoiding expensive repairs.
- **Keep a Maintenance Log:** Record oil changes, tire rotations, and other

maintenance activities for future reference and warranty claims. Knowledge is power (and excellent for your automobile karma!). Incorporating these basic car maintenance techniques into your daily routine improves your vehicle's performance and provides a safer driving experience on Massachusetts roads. Your dedication to vehicle maintenance enables you to travel the different landscapes of the Bay State with confidence and peace of mind. Safe travels!

Handling Emergencies

While we hope for a smooth journeys, being prepared for emergencies is an important component of safe driving. This part will provide you with the skills and information necessary to properly deal with unanticipated problems on Massachusetts roadways.

- **Be Calm:** It is critical to remain cool in an emergency. Take a deep breath, examine the issue, and make your choice with clear thinking.

- **Pull Over Safely:** If possible move your car to a safe area away from traffic. Use danger lights to alert other cars, and use emergency flares or triangles as needed.
- **Emergency Kit:** Maintain a well-stocked emergency kit in your car with basics such as a first aid kit, flashlight, jumper cables, blankets, and non-perishable food. These objects may be quite useful in a variety of scenarios.
- **Contact Emergency Services:** For major accidents or medical situations, dial 911 immediately. Please provide precise information about your location and the nature of the situation.
- **Flat Tire Blues:** Don't Let Deflation Deflate Your Spirit!" If you have a tire blowout, grab the steering wheel tightly, ease off the throttle, and bring the car to a

controlled halt. If you can safely change the tire, do so; otherwise, get help.

- **Evaluate the situation:** Is it safe to replace the tire yourself? If not, call roadside help or a reliable buddy with mechanical skills. If DIY is your thing, get your tools and a spare tire from the trunk.
- **Jack It Up (Safety!):** Locate the proper jacking points on your vehicle (if unclear, see your owner's manual). Secure the jack, release the lug nuts slightly while the tire remains on the ground, and then elevate the vehicle with the jack.
- **Swap those shoes:** Remove the flat tire fully and then install the spare. Tighten the lug nuts tightly in a star pattern (see your manual for the appropriate torque). Lower the vehicle, remove the jack, and double-check that the lug nuts are secure.
- **Don't Forget the Spare:** Remember that spare tires are just temporary fixes. Have your

flat tire fixed or replaced as quickly as possible.
- **Engine Overheating:** If the engine overheats, switch off the car and allow it to cool before opening the hood. Check coolant levels and add water as needed. Seek professional assistance if the situation persists.
- **Electrical breakdown:** In the event of an electrical breakdown, use danger lights to alert other vehicles. Stop safely and analyze the situation. If feasible, troubleshoot or get expert assistance.
- **Battery Issues:** If your battery dies, use jumper wires to start your car with help from another driver. Learn appropriate jump-starting practices.
- **Getting Stuck:** Avoid excessive acceleration that might cause the car to get stuck further. Place sand, gravel, or traction mats below the tires. Call for roadside assistance if necessary.

- **Accidents Happen:** Stay Safe and Clear! Prioritize safety during a collision. Check for injuries and call for medical assistance if necessary. Exchange information with other involved parties and report the incident to the police
- **Check for Injuries:** If someone is harmed, contact 911 immediately. Prioritize first assistance and medical care above everything else.
- **Secure the Scene:** Use your warning lights and emergency flares (if available) to alert other cars. If possible, move your vehicle slightly off the road to prevent more crashes.
- **Call for Assistance:** Contact the police and give detailed details about the accident location and any injuries. Except for the police, do not confess blame or disclose the circumstances of the collision.
- **Remain Calm and Cooperative:** Answer the police officers' inquiries honestly and

quietly. Follow their directions and avoid disputes. Remember that cooperation results in a seamless and safe conclusion to the matter.

- **Roadside Assistance:** Consider enrolling in a roadside assistance service. Access to expert assistance may help to resolve a variety of roadside concerns more quickly.
- **Know Your Location:** Always be mindful of your location, particularly in unfamiliar areas. When requesting help, offer correct information by using landmarks, road signs, or GPS.

Bonus Round: Emergency Preparedness Gems:
- **Emergency Kit Essentials:** Include a first-aid kit, water, non-perishable food, a flashlight, blankets, and a phone charger. It may not avoid an emergency, but it may make dealing with one far less stressful.
- **Know Your Limits:** Do not try unsafe repairs or manage circumstances that are

above your skill level. Call for assistance and let the specialists handle it. Remember: safety first!

- **Remain Positive and Focused:** Even in an emergency, being cool and level-headed may make a significant difference. Take deep breaths, concentrate on the work at hand, and believe that you can do it.

By being acquainted with these emergency response tactics, you will be better prepared to deal with unexpected obstacles on Massachusetts highways. Preparedness and a cool disposition can help you navigate situations and ensure your own and others' safety. Safe travels!

Driving in Construction Zones

Construction zones are a common sight along Massachusetts roadways, indicating ongoing work and improvements. However, these areas present specific challenges that require drivers to be cautious and follow special laws. In this section, we'll explore the rules and procedures for driving through construction zones safely.

- **Reduce Speed:** Adhere to posted speed restrictions in construction zones, which are often lower than regular limits. Slowing down enhances your capacity to respond to changing situations.
- **Follow Traffic Signs:** Pay close attention to construction zone signs, including reduced speed limits, lane closures, and detour directions. Following these signs is crucial for safely maneuvering through the construction area.
- **Merge Promptly:** When lanes merge due to construction, ensure a smooth transition. Avoid last-minute lane changes, which can disrupt traffic flow and create hazardous situations.
- **Maintain a Safe Following Distance:** Stay at least a safe distance behind the vehicle in

front of you. This provides plenty of time to respond to abrupt pauses or slowdowns in construction zones.

- **Stick to Designated Lanes:** Avoid driving in closed or blocked-off areas. Construction zones may have changing lane patterns, so staying in the correct lanes is essential for safety.
- **Be Cautious of Construction Workers:** Be aware of construction workers and equipment. Follow the designated work zone signs and be prepared to yield to construction vehicles.
- **Avoid Distractions:** Limit distractions such as using your phone or adjusting the radio. Construction zones demand your full attention, and inattentive driving may result in accidents.
- **Plan for Delays:** Construction zones may create delays, so adjust your journey time appropriately. Anticipate potential delays

due to lane closures, detours, or reduced speed restrictions.

- **Watch for Uneven Road Surfaces:** Be attentive to uneven road surfaces, temporary pavement, or changes in road conditions in construction zones. Adjust your driving style accordingly to maintain control.
- **Be Patient:** Exercise patience when driving through construction zones. Construction is temporary, and delays are often for the improvement of roadways. Allow extra time for your journey.
- **Obey Flaggers:** Follow flaggers' signals and directives in construction zones. Their instructions take precedence over regular traffic lights and signage.
- **Report Hazardous Circumstances:** Report any hazardous conditions or dangers in a construction zone to the relevant authorities. Your vigilance contributes to the

safety of both drivers and construction workers.

Bonus Round: Construction Zone Insider Tips:

- **Plan Your Trip:** Review traffic reports and explore alternative routes, especially during peak hours. Remember, avoiding the zone may save you time and stress.
- **Be Patient and Respectful:** Delays are inevitable in construction zones. Stay calm, avoid confrontational behavior, and remember that the workers are there to improve our roads for everyone.
- **Stay Alert and Focused:** Distractions such as using your phone or eating can be detrimental in the ever-changing environment of a construction site. Keep your focus on the road and your reflexes sharp.

Following these principles contributes to a safer driving experience in construction zones. When navigating these areas, exercise caution, follow the posted guidance, and maintain patience. Your responsible driving in construction zones ensures the safety of both you and those working to enhance our roads. Safe travels!

CHAPTER 6: SPECIAL DRIVING CONDITIONS

Welcome to Chapter 6, where we delve into the intricacies of driving under special conditions in Massachusetts.

Night Driving Safety Tips

In this section, we'll focus on the unique challenges and considerations for driving at night, ensuring you can navigate the roads safely when the sun goes down.

- **Proper Lighting:** Ensure all your vehicle's lights are functioning correctly, including headlights, taillights, and signal lights. Proper lighting is crucial for your visibility and that of other drivers.
- **Use Low Beams:** When driving at night, use low-beam headlights to avoid dazzling oncoming drivers. Dim the dashboard lights to prevent interior glare.

- **Reduce Speed:** Slow down when driving at night, especially in areas with limited visibility. Lowering your speed enhances your response time to unexpected obstacles or changes in road conditions.
- **Maintain a Safe Following Distance:** Keep a safe following distance from the vehicle ahead of you. This allows more time to respond to sudden stops or maneuvers.
- **Be Alert to Pedestrians:** Pedestrians may be less visible at night. Exercise extra caution at crosswalks and intersections, always giving pedestrians the right of way.
- **Avoid Overdriving Headlights:** Maintain a speed that permits you to stop within the distance lighted by your headlights. Overdriving your headlights might limit your response time.
- **Clean Your Windshield:** Keep your windshield clean inside and out. Glare from

dirt or smudges may hinder sight, particularly at night.

- **Watch for Wildlife:** Wildlife is more active at night, so exercise caution. Scan the roadside for reflecting eyes and reduce speed in areas with frequent animal crossings.
- **Limit Distractions:** Minimize distractions inside your car. Keep conversations brief, reduce phone usage, and focus on the road.
- **Use High Beams Wisely:** Use high beams on dark highways but dim them when approaching or following another vehicle. Pay attention to oncoming cars to avoid causing discomfort or glare.
- **Check Your Vision:** Ensure your vision is suitable for night driving. Regular eye check-ups and corrective lenses, if necessary, contribute to improved driving safety.
- **Give Your Eyes a Break:** Staring at headlights may strain your eyes and reduce your peripheral vision. Take breaks to blink

and focus on distant objects to refresh your eyes. Remember, well-rested eyes lead to safe driving.

- **Beware the Glare:** Oncoming headlights can temporarily blind you. Look slightly to the side of the road to preserve eyesight, and slow down to allow for extra response time. Anticipating glare helps you stay on target.
- **Watch for Shadows:** Keep an eye out for shadows created by street lights and headlights, especially around crosswalks and intersections. Pedestrians and cyclists may be hidden in the shadows.
- **Plan Stops in Well-Lit Places:** When making stops on your journey, choose well-lit areas. This enhances safety during rest stops.
- **Get Enough Rest:** Avoid driving when tired. Fatigue is a significant risk factor for nighttime accidents. Prioritize sleep before embarking on long journeys.

- **Caffeine Can Help (But Does Not Fix Fatigue):** A cup of coffee may provide a short boost, but it is not a substitute for adequate sleep. Don't rely solely on coffee to stay awake, and if you feel tired, pull over and take a nap. Remember, safety is more important than fatigue.
- **Engage Your Senses:** Sing along with music, open a window for fresh air, and keep your mind engaged. Avoid monotonous activities that can make you drowsy. Remember A stimulated mind remains alert.

Bonus Round: Nighttime Navigation Ninjas
- **Plan Your Route:** Stick to familiar routes at night. Use established roads or GPS navigation to avoid getting lost in unfamiliar darkness.
- **Park Strategically:** Choose well-lit parking lots, preferably near your destination. Be aware of your surroundings, and trust your

instincts if anything seems unsafe. A well-lit route is a safer one.

- **Be Patient:** Nighttime traffic can be unpredictable. Allow extra time for your journey and avoid aggressive driving. Patience conquers the nocturnal chaos.

Incorporating these principles into your nighttime driving habits enhances safety for you and others on Massachusetts highways. Night driving requires heightened awareness and intelligent precautions, ensuring that your journeys after dark are as safe as they are necessary. Safe travels.

Driving in Fog or Heavy Rain

As we study specific driving conditions in Massachusetts, it's crucial to address the unique challenges offered by fog and heavy rain. In this section, we'll guide you on getting through these weather conditions with the care and planning necessary for safe driving.

Driving in Fog:

- **Reduce Speed:** In foggy situations, significantly reduce your speed. This gives extra time to respond to barriers or other vehicles that may appear quickly.
- **Use Low Beams:** Utilize low-beam headlights to improve vision without causing glare or reflection in the fog. High brightness can spread light and lower vision.
- **Activate Fog Lights:** If your car is equipped with fog lights, turn them on. These lights are meant to cut through fog and provide better lighting for the road.
- **Increase Following Distance:** Maintain a wide following distance from the car in front of you. Fog can confuse senses, and a longer following distance improves safety.
- **Listen for Traffic:** Roll down your windows to listen for traffic, as vision may be limited. Sounds can alert you to the presence of other cars.

- **Stay on Designated Paths:** Stick to marked lanes and follow the road's edge or middle. This helps you stay on the right road and avoid moving into oncoming traffic.
- **Use Defrosters and Fans:** Keep your windshield clear by using defrosters to prevent freezing and fans to remove rain or mist. Clear vision is crucial in foggy circumstances.
- **Be Cautious at Intersections:** Approach intersections with caution. Cross-traffic may be challenging to see, so check all ways carefully before continuing.

Driving in Heavy Rain:

- **Slow Down:** Reduce your speed when driving in heavy rain. Wet roads can be slippery, and slowing down improves grip and control.
- **Turn On Headlights:** Turn on your headlights to improve vision, even during the daytime. This not only helps you see better

but also makes your car more noticeable to others.

- **Turn On Those Wipers!:** Don't drive blind! Adjust your wipers speed to match the rain strength, and remember, clear vision is key to safe driving.
- **Use Your Defroster:** Foggy windows are an accident ready to happen. Turn on your defroster and keep it going to maintain clear vision. Remember, good ventilation keeps your view bright!
- **Maintain Distance:** Increase your following distance from the car in front of you. Rain can decrease vision, and a longer following distance allows for better stopping.
- **Avoid Standing Water:** Steer clear of standing water on the road. Puddles may be deeper than they look, and driving through them can lead to hydroplaning.

- **Use Turn Signals Early:** Signal your plans well in advance, giving other cars more time to respond to your moves in reduced sight.
- **Be Wary of Hydroplaning:** If you hydroplane (lose traction on a wet surface), ease off the accelerator and turn in the direction you want to go. Avoid rapid moves.
- **Be Mindful of Spray:** Be prepared for water spray from other cars. Adjust your speed and use window wipers properly to keep clear vision.
- **Check Tires:** Ensure your tires are in good condition with proper wear depth. Hydroplaning is more likely to occur on worn-out tires.

Bonus Round: Weather Warrior Wisdom:

- **Plan Your Trip Wisely:** Check the weather forecast before going out. If possible, avoid driving during bad weather conditions. Remember, sometimes keeping put is the best choice.

- **Keep an Emergency Kit Handy:** Pack basics like blankets, water, non-perishable food, a flashlight, and a first-aid kit. You never know when you might need them in bad weather.
- **Stay Alert and Focused:** Avoid distractions like your phone or food. Pay close attention to the road and predict changes in weather conditions. Remember, a focused mind navigates storms better.

By adding these guidelines into your approach, you'll travel through fog and heavy rain in Massachusetts with heightened care and safety. Weather-related difficulties require a cautious and aware driving style, ensuring that your trips are safe, regardless of the circumstances. Safe travels!

Navigating Hills and Curves

As we delve into the intricacies of handling hills and curves on Massachusetts roads, it's crucial to equip yourself with valuable insights to enhance your driving skills in undulating terrains and winding paths.

Driving on Hills:

- **Maintain Speed Control:** Whether ascending or descending hills, strive for a consistent speed. Utilize your vehicle's transmission smartly to manage descents without relying solely on brakes.
- **Uphill Driving:** Accelerate gently before ascending a hill. Utilize lower gears to provide more power, preventing undue strain on your engine.
- **Downhill Driving:** When descending, opt for a lower gear to control speed. Avoid continuous braking to prevent overheating.
- **Be Mindful of Blind Summits:** Exercise caution approaching the crest of a hill, especially if visibility is hindered. Reduce speed and be ready for unexpected situations.

- **Yield to Uphill Traffic:** On narrow roads, while descending, yield to uphill traffic. Uphill vehicles typically have the right of way.

Driving Through Curves:

- **Adjust Speed Proactively:** Reduce speed before entering a curve rather than during the turn. Proactive speed adjustment enhances control.
- **Stay Centered in Your Lane:** Aim to remain centered in your lane when navigating curves. Avoid drifting towards the inside or outside edges of the road.
- **Look Ahead:** Keep your gaze focused on the road ahead, looking through the curve rather than fixating on the immediate turn. This aids in anticipating the road's trajectory.
- **Control Steering Smoothly:** Use smooth and controlled steering. Avoid abrupt or jerky movements, as they can impact vehicle stability.

- **Avoid Overbraking:** While reducing speed is crucial, refrain from excessive braking mid-curve. Brake before entering the curve if necessary and maintain a consistent speed.
- **Mind Road Signs:** Pay attention to warning signs indicating upcoming curves. These signs offer valuable insights into the turn's severity and recommended speeds.
- **Be Cautious in Adverse Weather:** Exercise heightened caution in adverse weather conditions when navigating hills and curves. Reduced visibility or slippery roads demand increased vigilance.
- **Use Turnouts Wisely:** On narrow, winding roads, utilize turnouts to allow faster-moving traffic to pass. Exhibit courtesy to fellow drivers sharing the road.

Bonus Round: Hill & Curve Champions' Wisdom:

- **Practice Makes Perfect (and Safe):** Practice your hill and curve driving skills on safe, open roads before facing major challenges. Confidence stems from experience!

- **Know Your Limits:** Don't exceed yourself or your vehicle's capabilities. If a hill or curve seems daunting, slow down, or consider an alternative route. Safety outweighs ego.
- **Respect the Road and Other Drivers:** Be a courteous driver! Share the road responsibly, anticipate others' actions, and yield when necessary. Kindness keeps the curves calm and the hills happy!

By incorporating these insights into your driving repertoire, you'll confidently navigate the unique challenges presented by hills and curves in Massachusetts. Mastering the art of hill and curve navigation enhances your driving experience, allowing you to enjoy the scenic beauty of the state's diverse landscapes. Safe travels!

Railroad Crossings

As we navigate through the unique driving conditions of Massachusetts, it is imperative to emphasize the safety procedures and regulations associated with a critical aspect of road travel – railroad crossings. In this section, we will provide comprehensive guidance on the necessary steps and precautions when approaching and crossing these intersections.

Approaching A Railroad Crossing:**

- **Be Alert:** Approach railroad crossings with extra caution. Look and listen for oncoming trains, particularly in low-visibility locations.
- **Recognize Warning Signs:** Pay attention to warning signals that indicate an impending train crossing. These signs provide critical information regarding the crossing's position and the necessity to prepare for an incoming train.

- **Activate Hazard Lights:** Use your hazard lights to notify other cars of the oncoming crossing. This is particularly critical if you're traveling slowly or coming to a halt.
- **Reduce Speed:** Slow down as you approach a railroad crossing. Adhering to stated speed limits allows you plenty of time to respond to signals and obstructions.
- **Check for Signals:** Look for flashing lights, warning bells, or gate arms at the crossing. These are triggered as a train approaches. Never try to cross if these signals are activated.
- **Listen for Train Horns:** Roll down your windows to hear incoming trains. Trains must blow their horns while approaching a crossing.

Crossing The Railroad Tracks:

- **Stop Behind The White Line:** Come to a full halt behind the white line or pavement markings, allowing sufficient clearance for the crossing gates.

- **Look Both Ways:** Check both ways before crossing the tracks, even if signs show all-clear. Trains may approach from both directions.
- **Avoid Stopping on Tracks:** Do not stop on railroad tracks. If you are stuck in traffic and are unable to remove the tracks entirely, wait till you can.
- **Wait for Gates to Rise:** If the crossing contains gate arms, wait for them to completely raise before going. Do not try to cross when the gates are still lowering or rising.
- **Be Aware of Numerous Tracks:** Some crossings have numerous tracks. Before continuing, ensure that all tracks are clear, since trains may be traveling on neighboring tracks.

- **Never Race a Train:** Never try to race or beat an oncoming train to the crossing. Trains move quicker than they look, and misjudging their speed may have serious repercussions.
- **Be Patient:** Maintain patience while waiting for a train to pass. Avoid attempting to navigate around lowered gates or barricades.

After Crossing:

- **Clear the Entire Crossing:** Ensure your entire vehicle has fully crossed the tracks before proceeding. Refrain from stopping on the tracks after crossing.
- **Be Cautious at Multiple Tracks:** Exercise extra caution at railroad crossings with multiple tracks. Confirm that all tracks are clear before proceeding.
- **Look and Listen Again:** Even after crossing, remain vigilant and attentive for any additional trains. Trains can approach from multiple directions.

- **Report Malfunctions:** If you encounter malfunctioning warning devices or other issues at a railroad crossing, promptly report them to the appropriate authorities.

Adherence to these safety practices at railroad crossings is critical for your own and others' safety on the road. Railroad crossings need vigilance, prudence, and strict respect for signals and laws. Following these principles contributes to a safer driving experience near train tracks in Massachusetts. Safe travels!

CHAPTER 7: MASSACHUSETTS TRAFFIC LAWS

Welcome to Chapter 7, where we embark on a comprehensive exploration of the legal framework that controls transportation in the magnificent state of Massachusetts. Understanding and following traffic regulations is not only a legal requirement, but also an important part of driving responsibly and safely. In this session, we'll look at the essential features of Massachusetts traffic regulations, giving you insight into how to efficiently navigate the legal terrain.

DUI/DWI Laws in Massachusetts

Understanding the rules and penalties of driving under the influence (DUI/DWI) is essential for safe driving in Massachusetts. Let's take a look at the legal framework and the consequences of driving while inebriated.

Know The Lingo:

- **DUI:** In Massachusetts, DUI, or Operating Under the Influence (OUI), is defined as having a blood alcohol content (BAC) of 0.08% or more.
- **DWI:** occurs when your ability to drive is affected by any substance, including alcohol, marijuana, prescription medicines, or illicit substances, even if your BAC is less than 0.08%.

Understand The Stakes:

- **Penalties:** for DUI/DWI include large fines, prison time, driver's license suspension or revocation, and possibly car seizure. Each transgression brings more severe sanctions.
- **Beyond Penalties:** DUI/DWI may lead to major accidents, injuries, and even death. You might be held responsible for financial and legal ramifications that harm you and others.

Know Your Limitations:

- **Personal Differences:** Alcohol affects people differently, and there is no universal "safe limit." Factors such as weight, gender, food consumption, and medications can influence your Blood Alcohol Concentration (BAC).
- **Avoid Risky Behavior:** Even a moderate BAC level can impair your judgment, coordination, and reaction time. Avoid engaging in risky behavior and recognize the importance of ensuring your safety and the well-being of fellow road users.

Blood Alcohol Concentration (BAC) Limits:

- In Massachusetts, the legal limit for blood alcohol concentration (BAC) is 0.08%. This implies that if a driver's BAC level equals or surpasses 0.08%, they are legally impaired.

- **Under 21:** For those under the age of 21, a stricter standard is implemented. Any Blood Alcohol Concentration (BAC) level of 0.02% or above is considered a violation of DUI laws, emphasizing the more rigorous criteria for underage drivers.

The consequences of DUI convictions:

A DUI conviction in Massachusetts has serious repercussions, including:

- **Fines:** DUI convictions sometimes result in large penalties, which may vary depending on criteria such as prior crimes and degree of intoxication.
- **License Suspension:** A DUI conviction typically results in the suspension of the driver's license. The length of the suspension varies, with longer periods for repeat offenses.
- **Mandatory Alcohol Education Programs:** Offenders are often obliged to attend mandatory alcohol education

programs designed to raise awareness about the hazards of intoxicated driving.

- **Probation:** Probation may be imposed, during which time the person must follow the court's specified requirements, such as frequent check-ins with a probation officer.
- **Ignition Interlock Devices:** In rare situations, the court may order the installation of an ignition interlock device in the offender's car. This technology detects BAC levels and allows the car to start only when the driver is sober.
- **Imprisonment:** Individuals convicted of DUI may face jail time, depending on the severity of the crime and any past DUI history. Jail sentences might last from a few days to many months.

Legal Procedure:

- The legal procedure for DUI charges often includes arrest, court hearings, and possible plea bargaining. Individuals charged with

DUI should obtain legal advice to understand the complexity of the judicial system.

Refusal to Submit to Testing:

- Declining to undergo a chemical test for BAC level assessment can result in additional consequences, such as an automatic suspension of the driver's license.

Bonus Round for Responsible Road Warrior Wisdom:

- **Educate Yourself:** Learn about the current DUI/DWI laws and punishments in Massachusetts. Making safe decisions requires knowledge.
- **Speak Up:** Do not be hesitant to confront friends or family members who intend to drive under the influence. Your voice may help avoid a catastrophe.
- **Set a good example:** Demonstrate responsible driving habits and actively

support road safety. Your actions carry weight and contribute to a safer driving culture.

It is critical to understand that the implications of DUI convictions go beyond the legal penalties. A DUI record may have long-term consequences for work possibilities, insurance prices, and personal well-being. Responsible and sober driving is more than just a legal requirement; it is a commitment to the safety of oneself and others on the road. Always designate a sober driver or use an alternate mode of transportation if you are inebriated. Safe travels!

Seat Belts and Child Restraint Laws

Understanding and complying with seat belt and child restraint laws is critical to ensure the safety of all vehicle passengers. In Massachusetts, these restrictions are in place to reduce the possibility of harm in the case of an accident. Let's look at seat belt and kid restraint rules in order to encourage safe and responsible driving.

Seat Belt Requirements:

All occupants of a motor vehicle must wear a seatbelt in Massachusetts. The main points include:

- **Everyone on board buckles up:** No exceptions! Massachusetts law requires all passengers, regardless of age or seating position, to wear seat belts correctly at all times while the vehicle is moving.
- **Driver Responsibility:** It is the driver's responsibility to ensure that all passengers, regardless of age or seating position, are properly secured with seat belts.
- **Front Seat passengers:** All passengers in the front seats must always wear seat belts.
- **Rear Seat Occupants:** All passengers under the age of 13 must wear seat belts or be secured in an approved child restraint device while sitting in the vehicle's back seat.

- **Penalties for Non-Compliance:** Failure to comply with seat belt requirements may result in penalties and points against the driver's record.

Child Passenger Safety

Child restraint rules are intended to offer proper protection to children depending on their age, weight, and height. Here are the important features:

- **Infants and Toddlers (Under 5 Years Old):** Children under the age of 5 and weighing less than 40 pounds must use a federally authorized child passenger restraint device.
- **Booster Seats (Ages 5-12 or under 57 inches tall):** Children ages 5 to 12 or under 57 inches tall must use a booster seat until they meet the height or age requirement to wear a seat belt alone.
- **Seat Belt Usage (Over 12 or 57 Inches Tall):** Children over 12 or 57 inches tall may wear a seat belt without a booster seat.

- **Penalties for Noncompliance:** Violations of kid restraint rules may result in fines and points on the driver's license.

Enforcement and Safety Impact:
- Law enforcement enforces seat belt and child restraint laws to ensure safety. In addition to meeting legal requirements, utilizing seat belts and suitable kid restraints significantly minimizes the risk of injury or death in the case of an accident.

Bonus round: Safe Journey Gems

- **Check Your Car Seats Frequently:** Expired or damaged car seats might endanger safety. Follow the manufacturer's directions to keep yours up-to-date and in excellent condition.
- **Practice makes perfect:** Help youngsters get comfortable with their car seats and practice buckling up on their own. It becomes a habit that increases safety awareness.

- **Lead by Example:** Always wear a seatbelt and inspire others to follow suit. Consistency and positive reinforcement help to create a safe culture.

Responsible and safe driving entails not just following traffic regulations, but also assuring the safety of all passengers. Drivers play an important role in making roads safer for everyone by adhering to seat belt and child restraint requirements. Buckle up and secure your valuable cargo; it is a simple but effective technique to save lives on the road. Have a safe trip!

Mobile Phone and Texting Regulations

As we go through the complexities of safe driving in Massachusetts, it is important to be aware of the laws governing mobile phone usage and texting while driving. Understanding and adhering to these standards makes roads safer for everyone. Let's look into the specifics of mobile phone and texting regulations in the state.

- **Handheld Device Ban:** Massachusetts has strictly prohibited the use of portable electronic devices while driving a car. This includes texting, calling, and any manual manipulation of the device.
- **Hands Free Requirement:** To encourage safer driving habits, Massachusetts law requires the use of hands-free technology for phone conversations while driving. Drivers must make or receive calls using voice instructions, Bluetooth technology, or other hands-free solutions.
- **Texting ban:** Texting while driving is strictly forbidden in Massachusetts. This applies to authoring, sending, and reading electronic communications such as text messages, emails, and instant messaging.

The consequences of violations:

Violating mobile phone and texting restrictions may have serious repercussions.
- **Fines:** Individuals found using portable electronics or texting while driving may be fined. The cost fluctuates according to the number of crimes.
- **License points:** Violations usually result in the addition of points to the driver's record. Accumulating too many points within a certain time frame might result in license suspension.
- **License suspension:** In certain cases, multiple infractions or major crimes may result in the suspension of a driver's license.

Exceptions to the Ban:

There are specific situations where the use of handheld devices is allowed:
- **Emergency Situations:** In an emergency, you may use a portable device to call emergency services.

- **Stationary Vehicle:** The prohibition does not apply if the vehicle is stopped and not in active traffic.

Enforcement and Road Safety:

- Law enforcement agencies enforce mobile phone and texting prohibitions to improve road safety. Distracted driving is a danger, and following these regulations is critical for avoiding accidents and protecting the safety of all road users.

Take the Pledge to Drive Distraction-Free:

- Promoting a culture of distraction-free driving begins with individual dedication. Drivers who promise to drive distraction-free help to make the road safer for everyone. Remember that every call or text can wait; prioritize safety and keep focused on the road. Safe travels!

Bonus Round: Mobile Savvy Tips.

- **Plan Your Route:** Before you begin driving, set up your navigation system to prevent the temptation to fidget with your phone while driving.
- **Let them know you're driving:** Inform friends and relatives that you will be unavailable while driving but you will reply to messages once you arrive.
- **Be a Role Model:** Set a positive example for other drivers and passengers by putting your phone aside and paying attention to the road.

Parking Regulations

Understanding the parking laws and regulations in Massachusetts is critical for preserving street order and making the most use of available parking spots. Whether in bustling urban areas or quieter neighborhoods, following parking standards helps to improve traffic flow and creates a safer environment for everyone. Let's look at some of the important components of the state's parking rules.

Metered parking:

In metered parking zones, drivers must follow particular laws to avoid penalties and guarantee that places are available for others. **Key points include**:

- **Time Limit:** Metered parking spots often contain time constraints. Drivers must leave the spot within the time limit to avoid fines.

- **Payment Requirements:** Make sure the meter is paid for the duration of your planned stay. Familiarize yourself with acceptable payment methods for the meter.
- **Metre Hours:** Be careful of the hours when meters are enforced. Some meters may have different restrictions on the nights, weekends, or holidays.

Street parking:

Street parking restrictions vary, and learning the local requirements might help you avoid penalties and fines. **Key factors include:**

- **Designated Hours:** Parking hours may be set on certain streets. Check for signage showing acceptable parking hours.
- **Residential Permit Parking:** Certain areas may need a residential parking permit. Non-residents who do not have permission may be subject to restrictions or time limitations.
- **Street Cleaning Days:** Be informed of any planned street cleanings. Parking on the roadway during scheduled cleaning periods may result in fines or towing.

Handicapped parking:

Respect for disabled parking places is both a legal and moral requirement. **Key points include:**

- **Permit Display:** Only cars with valid handicapped parking permits are allowed in allocated areas.

- **Penalties for Violations:** Unauthorized usage of disabled parking spots is strictly forbidden and may result in severe penalties.

Enforcement and Penalty:

- Parking laws are strictly enforced, and breaches may result in penalties, fines, or towing. Check for parking restrictions signs regularly, and keep an eye out for any changes in regulations.

Parking Applications and Technology:

- In many cities, parking applications give real-time information on available spots, payment methods, and parking limitations. Using this technology may assist in streamlining the parking procedure and reduce violations.

Community Cooperation:

- Respecting parking regulations is a common duty. By following standards, drivers help to create a more orderly and accessible parking environment for everyone.

Bonus Round: Parking Power-ups:

- **Know Your Zone:** Familiarize yourself with the parking laws in your neighborhood and popular places. Knowledge is power—especially when it comes to avoiding penalties!
- **Read the Signs Every Time:** Do not presume you understand what a sign signifies! Always read and understand any parking limitations before leaving your vehicle.
- **Plan your parking:** Consider parking while planning your trip, particularly in congested regions, public transit or ride-sharing services may be more viable choices.

Staying knowledgeable about parking restrictions is an important element of driving responsibly. Whether in urban or suburban areas, following the guidelines ensures that parking spots are utilized effectively and securely. Drive responsibly, park carefully, and help to improve traffic flow in Massachusetts. Safe travels!

CHAPTER 8: DRIVER'S RESPONSIBILITIES

In Chapter 8, we explore the fundamental duties that come with being a driver in Massachusetts. Adhering to these responsibilities ensures not only your safety but also contributes to the overall well-being of the road environment. Let's delve into the most crucial aspects of a driver's responsibilities.

Reporting Accidents

Being involved in a traffic accident can be challenging experience, but knowing the proper procedures and duties is critical for everyone involved. In Massachusetts, it's crucial to react appropriately and promptly after a traffic accident. Here's a detailed description of the procedures and requirements if you find yourself in this situation:

- **Prioritize Safety:** Put your safety and that of others first. If possible, move vehicles to a safe location and turn on the warning lights.

- **Check for Injuries:** Evaluate the safety of all those involved. If there are injuries, call for medical assistance immediately.
- **Exchange Information:** Share important information with the other parties involved, including names, addresses, phone numbers, insurance information, and vehicle registration numbers.
- **Document The Scene:** Photograph the accident scene, including vehicle positions, damages, and relevant road conditions. These images may be useful for insurance claims and legal proceedings.
- **Contact Law Enforcement:** In certain circumstances, contact law enforcement to report the accident, especially in cases of injury, significant property damage, or disputes among parties.
- **File an Accident Report:** In Massachusetts, file an accident report with

the Registry of Motor Vehicles (RMV) within five days if the accident resulted in injury, death, or property damage exceeding $1,000.

- **Cooperate with Authorities:** Fully cooperate with law enforcement officers on-site. Provide the right information and follow their instructions.
- **Seek Witness Information:** If there were witnesses, obtain their contact information. Witness accounts may be useful in insurance claims or legal proceedings.
- **Do Not Admit Blame:** Avoid admitting fault or using phrases that might be seen as an admission of guilt. Let insurers and authorities assess culpability based on facts.
- **Inform Your Insurance Company:** Contact your insurance company promptly about the accident. Provide clear and detailed information to expedite the claims process.

- **Seek Legal Assistance if Necessary:** In case of disputes or legal issues, consider seeking legal advice to understand your rights and responsibilities.

Remember that reporting accident promptly and correctly is not only a legal obligation but also essential for filing insurance claims and resolving disputes. By acting appropriately, you contribute to a more efficient post-accident process and help preserve the safety and well-being of everyone involved. Safe travels!

Insurance Requirements

In Massachusetts, maintaining adequate insurance coverage is an essential component of safe driving. Understanding insurance requirements ensures that you follow the law and, more importantly, that you and other road users are protected in the event of an accident. Here is a detailed description of the insurance requirements for drivers in the Bay State:

- **Minimum Liability Coverage:** Massachusetts law mandates drivers to have a minimum level of liability insurance to cover injuries or property damage for which they are legally responsible.
- **Minimum Coverage Limits:** The minimum liability coverage limits in Massachusetts are:

  $20,000 per person for bodily injury

  $40,000 per accident for bodily injury (if multiple people are injured)

  $5,000 per accident for property damage
- **Personal Injury Protection (PIP):** Massachusetts is a no-fault state, requiring Personal Injury Protection (PIP) coverage. PIP covers medical expenses, lost wages, and necessary services for you and your passengers, regardless of fault in an accident.
- **Uninsured Motorist Coverage:** Uninsured Motorist (UM) coverage is required in Massachusetts, this coverage protects you in

the event of an accident with an uninsured driver or a hit-and-run situation.

- **Underinsured Motorist Coverage:** Underinsured Motorist (UIM) coverage is also mandatory, this coverage applies if you are in an accident with a driver whose insurance coverage is insufficient to cover your damages.
- **Evidence of Insurance:** Massachusetts law requires drivers to carry proof of insurance in their vehicles at all times, which may be needed during a traffic stop or after an accident.
- **Penalty for Lack of Insurance:** Failure to maintain required insurance coverage may result in penalties such as fines, license suspension, and the submission of an SR-22 (Certificate of Financial Responsibility).
- **Optional Coverages:** While the aforementioned coverages are required, drivers may choose additional coverages such

as Collision and Comprehensive insurance for more protection against physical damage to their vehicles.

- **Periodic Insurance Verification:** The Massachusetts Registry of Motor Vehicles (RMV) conducts periodic insurance verification checks. If selected, drivers must provide documentation of insurance or face penalties.

Understanding and complying with these insurance regulations is critical for safe driving in Massachusetts. Adequate insurance coverage not only fulfills legal requirements but also provides financial protection for you and others on the road. Regularly review your insurance coverage to ensure it meets the state's minimum requirements and adequately covers your needs. Safe travels!

Understanding Points and Penalties

In Massachusetts, the point system is utilized to monitor and penalize drivers for various traffic offenses. Understanding how the system works is crucial, as accumulating points may have serious ramifications for your driving record and rights. Here is a comprehensive guide to the points system and related fines for traffic infractions in the Bay State:

- **Points System Overview:** Massachusetts assigns points for certain traffic violations. The more serious the offense, the higher the point value.
- **Common Traffic Violations and Points:** Examples of typical traffic offenses and their related points are:
  Speeding: 2-5 pts.
  Running a red light gives you 2 points.
  Failure to yield: 3 points.

Failure to signal: 2 points.

Reckless driving: 5 points.

- **Point Accrual:** Conviction for a traffic infringement adds points to your driving record. The date of the offense determines when these points are added.
- **Implications of Points:** Accumulating points on your driving record can result in various consequences, including:

  Increased insurance prices.

  License suspension.

  Mandatory attendance in driver retraining programs.
- **License Suspension Thresholds:** The Massachusetts Registry of Motor Vehicles (RMV) may suspend your driver's license if you accumulate:

  5 to 6 points during 12 months.

  7 to 8 points during 24 months.

  9 or more points during 24 months.

- **Driver Retraining Programs:** Drivers who accumulate a certain number of points may need to attend a retraining program. Completing this program may result in a reduction of up to four points on your driving record.
- **Safe Driving Insurance Plan (SDIP):**** The Safe Driver Insurance scheme is a merit rating system that determines your auto insurance premiums based on your driving record. Accumulating points may lead to higher insurance prices.
- **Appeal Process:** If you believe a traffic offense was incorrectly assigned to you, you may appeal the ticket. For further information on the appeals procedure, contact the Massachusetts RMV.
- **Period of Point Consideration:** Points are assessed for insurance and license suspension during a defined term. Typically, points stay on your driving record for six years.

Understanding the point system is critical for all Massachusetts drivers. Responsible and careful driving helps to avoid collecting points, maintain a clean driving record, and reduce the possibility of fines. Check your driving record regularly, be aware of your point status, and take proactive efforts to ensure that you drive safely and without incurring any penalties. Safe travels!

Handling Traffic Tickets

Receiving a traffic tickets may be stressful, but knowing the procedure in Massachusetts allows drivers to negotiate the issue effectively. Here's a step-by-step approach that will help you manage traffic tickets and make educated decisions:

- **Review the Ticket:** Examine all information on the ticket, including the offense, location, and fine amount. Ensure that the information is correct.

- **Understand Your Alternatives:** In Massachusetts, you normally have three alternatives for dealing with a traffic ticket.
Pay your fine.
Suggest a hearing and contest the ticket.
Appeal the ticket if you disagree with the judge's ruling.
- **Payment Options:** If you choose to admit responsibility, you may pay the fine online, by mail, or in person at the specified court. Ensure that payment is completed within the stated term to avoid additional fines.
- **Contesting the Ticket:** If you feel the ticket is unfair or erroneous, you have the right to dispute it. Contesting a ticket entails pleading not guilty and presenting your argument to a court.
- **Requesting a Hearing:** Request a hearing to state your case and challenge the ticket. This option allows you to present evidence,

ask witnesses, and defend your case before a magistrate or court.

- **Prepare for the Hearing:** If you want to challenge the ticket or seek a hearing, preparation is essential. Gather any relevant proof, such as images, witness statements, or documentation, to support your claim.
- **Attend the Hearing:** Arrive in court on time. Present your argument straightforwardly and succinctly, including any facts or witnesses to support your defense.
- **Court's Ruling:** Following hearing your case, the court will make a ruling. If proven not guilty, the ticket may be dismissed. If found guilty, the court will impose any appropriate fines or punishments.
- **Appeal Process:** If you disagree with the judge's ruling, you have the right to appeal within a certain deadline. Consult the court

for further information on the appeals procedure.

- **Consider Legal Counsel:** In complex cases or if facing serious consequences, consider getting legal advice or hire an attorney to guide you through the legal procedure.
- **Comply with Court Orders:** Ensure prompt compliance with any fines or penalties imposed. Failure to pay penalties or comply with court-ordered obligations may result in further repercussions, including license suspension.

To navigate the traffic ticket procedure in Massachusetts, you must first understand your rights and duties. Whether you decide to pay the fine, challenge the ticket, or seek a hearing, being well-informed and prepared improves your ability to make sound judgments. Always act swiftly to fulfill deadlines and follow judicial processes. Safe travels!

CHAPTER 9: COMMERCIAL DRIVER'S LICENSE (CDL)

This chapter provides a comprehensive exploration of Commercial Driver's Licenses (CDLs), providing a comprehensive guide to the specific requirements and regulations for aspiring commercial drivers in Massachusetts

Overview of CDL Requirements

Obtaining a Commercial Driver's License (CDL) in Massachusetts involves meeting specific standards designed to ensure that prospective commercial drivers are adequately equipped and qualified for the responsibilities of professional driving. Here's a comprehensive overview of the major requirements:

Age Requirements:
- CDL applicants must be at least 18 years old for intrastate driving (within the state's borders).

- For interstate driving, the minimum age requirement is 21 years old (across state lines).

Driving Record:
- A clean driving record is essential requirement for obtaining a CDL.
- Certain transgressions, such as major traffic violations or DUI convictions, may disqualify applicants.

Medical Examination:
- CDL applicants must undergo a medical examination by a recognized practitioner.
- This examination evaluates the applicant's physical fitness to ensure they meet the health requirements for commercial driving.

Knowledge Exams:
- CDL applicants must pass knowledge exams to demonstrate their understanding of commercial driving laws and regulations.

- These examinations assess general knowledge, specialized endorsements (where applicable), and air brakes.

Skills Tests:
- Practical tests assess the applicant's safe operation of a commercial vehicle.
- The skills tests includes a pre-trip check, basic vehicle control, and an on-road driving test.

Endorsements (if applicable):
- Applicants may need additional endorsements based on their intended commercial driving type.
- Common endorsements include Hazardous Materials (Hazmat), Passenger, Tanker, and others.

Restrictions:
- A CDL may include limits that restrict the kind of vehicle or circumstances under which the driver may operate.

Meeting these prerequisites is an essential step in obtaining a CDL in Massachusetts. Aspiring commercial drivers should familiarize themselves with these requirements, ensuring that they are well-prepared and competent to pursue a career in professional driving. By following these requirements, drivers help to create a safer and more controlled commercial driving environment on Massachusetts highways. Safe travels on your way to becoming a professional commercial driver!

Endorsements and Restrictions for Commercial Drivers Licenses (CDL)

Commercial Driver's Licenses (CDLs) in Massachusetts may be customized with endorsements and may be subject to certain limitations depending on the type of commercial driving a person wishes to engage in. Understanding these endorsements and limits is critical for adapting a CDL to specific professional driving requirements. Let's look at the various CDL endorsements and restrictions:

Endorsements: Expanding Your Commercial Driving Horizons

Hazardous Materials (Hazmat):
- **Purpose:** Enables drivers to carry hazardous substances.
- **Requirements:** Must pass a specific knowledge exam and a federal background check.

Passenger Endorsement:
- **Purpose:** Allows drivers to transport passengers in a commercial vehicle.
- **Requirement:** Involves a written exam and a skills test for passenger transportation.

Tanker Endorsement:
- **Purpose:** Allows drivers to carry liquid or gaseous products in bulk.
- **Requirements:** Includes a written exam to evaluate knowledge of safe tanker operation.

Double/Triple Trailer Endorsement:
- **Purpose:** Enables drivers to operate vehicles with two or three trailers.
- **Requirements:** Must pass a written exam demonstrating understanding of pulling several trailers.

School Bus Endorsement:
- **Purpose:** Required for drivers who operate school buses.
- **Requirements:** Additional testing is required for the operation of school buses.

Restrictions: Limitations Designed for Specific Conditions

Air Brake Restriction (L):
- **Indication:** Placed on a CDL if the driver failed the air brake knowledge test or skills test in a vehicle equipped with air brakes.
- **Effect:** Restricts the driver from driving vehicles with air brakes.

Automatic Transmission Restriction (E):
- **Indication:** Applies if the driver performed the skills test in a vehicle with an automatic transmission.
- **Effect:** Restricts the driver to vehicles that have automatic gearboxes.

Interstate (Outside Massachusetts) Restriction (K):
- **Indication:** Applies if the driver passed the test in a vehicle with air brakes and plans to drive solely in Massachusetts.
- **Effect:** Restricts the driver to intrastate (within-state) actions.

Understanding endorsements and limits is critical for ensuring that a CDL matches the precise driving responsibilities that a commercial driver intends to undertake. Whether delivering hazardous commodities, people, or operating specialty vehicles, the appropriate endorsements increase a CDL holder's adaptability and employability.

Meanwhile, limits indicate certain requirements or constraints that drivers must follow. By mastering these characteristics, commercial drivers may customize their licenses to their professional driving goals. Safe travels on the routes for specialist commercial driving!

CDL Test Procedures

Obtaining a Commercial Driver's License (CDL) in Massachusetts requires a series of rigorous testing methods intended to examine a candidate's knowledge, abilities, and competence to drive commercial vehicles safely. Here's a thorough guide to help you understand the testing procedures:

Knowledge Tests: Building a Foundation of Comprehension

General Knowledge Test:
- **Purpose:** To assess comprehension of basic commercial driving laws and regulations.

- **Content:** Includes topics such as vehicle inspection, basic control, and on-road driving.

Endorsement Tests (if applicable):
- **Purpose:** Evaluates knowledge in specialist areas such as hazardous materials (Hazmat) or passenger transportation.
- **Content:** Focuses on the unique criteria for each endorsement.

Skills Tests: Demonstrating Practical Competence

Pre-trip Inspection:
- **Purpose:** Validates a driver's competence to examine a commercial vehicle for safety and operation.
- **Content:** Involves a thorough examination of the vehicle's components and systems.

Basic Vehicle operation:
- **Purpose:** Assesses the driver's ability to operate the vehicle in different scenarios.

- **Content:** Requires backing, turning, and parking techniques.

On-Road Driving:
- **Purpose:** Assesses a driver's competence in realistic driving situations.
- **Content:** Includes handling traffic, crossroads, and reacting to road signs.

Behind-the-Wheel Training to Improve Practical Skills

Training Period:
- **Purpose:** Gives applicants hands-on experience with a qualified CDL instructor.
- **Content:** Provides on-road instruction, vehicle operating practice, and advice on various driving circumstances.

CDL Issuance: Obtaining a Commercial Driver's License

Successful Completion:
- **Purpose:** Acknowledges individuals who have passed both knowledge and skills tests.

- **Content:** Includes the issue of a CDL with the appropriate endorsements.

Endorsement Specific Requirements: Specialized Competence

Hazmat Endorsement:
- **Purpose:*** Ensures applicants are prepared to carry hazardous goods.
- **Content:** Additional background and fingerprint checks are required.

Passenger Endorsement:
- **Purpose:** To ensures safe passenger transportation.
- **Content:** Contains a skills test focusing on passenger transportation.

Navigating the CDL examination processes requires a dedication to study, practical skill improvement, and full awareness of both general and endorsement-specific regulations. Aspiring commercial drivers should approach the testing procedure with devotion and a focus on safety, ensuring that they are fully prepared for the obligations that come with professional driving. Best wishes in your endeavor to earn a commercial driver's license in Massachusetts!

Safety Regulations for Commercial Drivers

Commercial drivers in Massachusetts must adhere to safety regulations that prioritize highway safety and high standards. Commercial drivers in Massachusetts play an important part in ensuring the safety and integrity of the state's roads. Adhering to specific safety requirements is not only a legal necessity, but also demonstrates a dedication to the safety of all road users. Let's look at the important safety requirements that commercial drivers must rigorously follow in Massachusetts:

Hours of Service (HOS): Managing Driving Hours for Well-Rested Drivers

- **Purpose:** Reduces driver tiredness and improves road safety.

- **Regulations:** Hours of service restrict daily driving time.
- Rest intervals are necessary, and there is a minimum off-duty duration between shifts.
- Enforces a weekly driving limit to avoid tiredness.

Weight Limits: Preserving Infrastructure and Road Quality

- **Purpose:** To prevent damage to road infrastructure and preserve overall road quality.
- **Regulations:** Commercial vehicles must meet weight restrictions specified by Massachusetts transportation authorities.
- Vehicles that are overweight or inappropriately loaded may be fined and penalized.

Vehicle Inspections: Ensuring Safe and Roadworthy Commercial Vehicles

- **Purpose:** Identifies and resolves any safety concerns with commercial vehicles quickly.

- **Regulations:** Requires frequent inspections of commercial vehicles, including pre-trip checks performed by drivers.
- Outlines roadworthiness standards, covering aspects such as brakes, lights, tires, and general vehicle condition.

Transportation of Hazardous Materials (Hazmat): Stringent Safety Guidelines

- **Purpose:** Minimizes hazards to public safety by ensuring safe transportation of hazardous materials.
- **Regulations:** Drivers transporting hazardous items must undergo specific training and get an endorsement.
- Establishes strict guidelines for labeling, packing, and handling hazardous cargo.

Compliance with Traffic rules: Upholding Standard Road Regulations

- **Purpose:** Encourages road safety and adherence to traffic rules.

- **Regulation:** Commercial drivers must follow all traffic laws, including speed limits, signals, and right-of-way regulations.
- Violations may result in fines, penalties, and possibly license suspension.

Drug and Alcohol Testing: Ensuring Sober and Alert Commercial Drivers

- **Purpose:** To provides a drug and alcohol-free environment for commercial drivers.
- **Regulations:** Commercial drivers must be tested for drugs and alcohol before employment, at random, after an accident, and on reasonable suspicion.
- Non-compliance may lead to suspension or disqualification.

Adhering to these safety laws is both a legal requirement and a commitment to maintaining high levels of professionalism and accountability. Commercial drivers in Massachusetts are critical contributors to road safety, and by adhering to these standards, they help to maintain the integrity of the state's transportation system. Safe travels on Massachusetts roadways!

CHAPTER 10: ADDITIONAL RESOURCES

As you embark on your journey to becoming a responsible and knowledgeable driver in Massachusetts, this chapter offers a comprehensive collection of supplementary information. These resources are designed to complement your understanding of Massachusetts driving legislation and provide further assistance. Let's explore:

Useful Websites and Contact Information

As you go through into the intricacies of Massachusetts driving, this section provides a curated selection of essential websites and contact information to serve as your go-to resources for additional assistance. Stay connected, informed, and empowered on your path as a responsible driver.

Helpful Websites: Navigating the Online Landscape for Information

Massachusetts Registry of Motor Vehicles (RMV)

- **Website:** [www.mass.gov/rmv]
- **Purpose:** Access official RMV information, online services, and stay up-to-date on driving rules.

Massachusetts Department of Transportation (MassDOT)

- **Website:** [www.mass.gov/orgs/massachusetts-department-of-transportation]
- **Purpose:** Stay informed about transportation projects, road conditions, and statewide initiatives.

National Highway Traffic Safety Administration (NHTSA)

- **Website:** [www.nhtsa.gov]
- **Purpose:** Discover comprehensive safety information, car recalls, and educational resources.

Insurance Information Institute (III):**
- **Website:** [www.iii.org]
- **Purpose:** Learn about insurance fundamentals, coverage alternatives, and industry developments.

AAA Northeast:
- **Website:** [northeast.aaa.com]
- **Purpose:** Get driving advice, travel information, and unique member privileges.

Contact Information: Interacting with Relevant Authorities

RMV Customer Service:
- **Phone:** 857-368-8000, 857-368-9500
- **Purpose:** Handle direct queries, schedule appointments, and provide general help.

MassDOT Contact Center:
- **Phone:** 857-368-4636, (877) 623-6846
- **Purpose:** Gather information on transportation projects, road closures, and travel warnings.

NHTSA Hotline:
- **Phone:** 888-327-4236
- **Purpose:** Report car issues, make complaints, and get access to safety information.

Emergency Services:
- **Emergency:** 911, +1 866-374-3473
- **Purpose:** Call for emergency, accident, or urgent help.

Local Law Enforcement Agencies:
- **Phone:** +1 978-794-5900, +1 617-796-2100, +1 508-676-8511
- **Purpose:** Collect non-emergency contact information for local police agencies.

Glossary of Terms

This section includes a glossary of common driving phrases to help you comprehend the language used in the Massachusetts Driver's Manual and other resources.

A

Acceleration Lane:

Definition: A designated lane for gradually increasing speed before safely merging with existing traffic.

Adverse Weather Conditions:

Definition: Unfavorable weather conditions, such as rain, snow, or fog, that may impact driving conditions.

B

Blind Spot:

Definition: An area surrounding a vehicle that cannot be seen in mirrors, requiring a shoulder check for safe lane changes.

Brake Fade:

Definition: Reduced braking effectiveness due to overheating of the brakes after prolonged use.

C

Carriageway:

Definition: The paved section of the road designed for automobile usage, excluding shoulders.

Crosswalk:

Definition: A designated space for pedestrians to cross the road, usually marked with painted lines.

D

Defensive Driving:

Definition: A proactive driving style that prioritizes predicting and avoiding potential risks.

DUI/DWI:

Definition: Driving Under the Influence/Driving While Intoxicated refers to driving a vehicle under the influence of alcohol or drugs.

E

Endorsement:

Definition: Additional qualification on a driver's license for operating certain vehicles or transporting specified products.

F

Fog Line:

Definition: A painted line along the road's edge that marks the border between the traffic lane and the shoulder.

Freeway:
Definition: A high-speed, controlled-access roadway featuring on/off ramps.

H
High Occupancy Vehicle (HOV) Lane:
Definition: A reserved lane for cars with a minimal number of people, usually to encourage carpooling.

Hydroplaning:
Definition: Loss of traction on wet roads, resulting in tires riding on a thin coating of water.

I
Intersection:
Definition: A point where two or more roads meet or cross.

J
Jersey Barrier:
Definition: A concrete barrier that separates lanes of traffic or protects against oncoming cars.

K
K-turn:
Definition: A three-point turn where a driver turns the car around using a succession of left and right turns.

L

Lane Departure Warning (LDW):

Definition: An advanced driving-assistance system that warns the driver if the car unexpectedly wanders out of its lane.

Learner's Permit:

Definition: A temporary permit allowing individuals to practice driving under the supervision of a licensed adult before obtaining a full driver's license.

M

Merge:

Definition: Consolidating two lanes of traffic into one, usually while approaching a highway or expressway.

Motorcycle Lane-Splitting:

Definition: The act of riding a motorbike between lanes of slow-moving or stopped traffic.

N

No-Zone:

Definition: Areas around a large vehicle, such as a truck or bus, where the driver has little or no view.

No-responsibility Insurance:

Definition: A system in which a driver's insurance covers their injuries and damages regardless of responsibility in an accident.

O

Off-Ramp:

Definition: A ramp that enables cars to leave a highway or expressway.

Overhead Clearance:

Definition: The vertical space for a vehicle to safely travel under structures such as bridges or overpasses.

P

Parallel Parking:

Definition: Parking a car parallel to the curb or road, usually between two other parked automobiles.

Pedestrian Crosswalk:

Definition: A defined location on a road where pedestrians have the right of way to cross.

Q
Quick Clearance:
Definition: Immediate clearance of cars from non-injury traffic incidents to decrease congestion and increase safety.

R
Roundabout:
Definition: A circular crossroads with traffic moving continually in one direction around a central island.

Road Rage:
Definition: Drivers displaying aggressive or violent conduct in response to perceived infractions or frustrations on the road.

S
Safe Following Distance:
Definition: The recommended spacing between cars for acceptable response time and accident prevention.

Shoulder:
Definition: The space on the side of the road, outside of the traffic lane, reserved for emergency stops or parking.

T

Traffic Calming:

Definition: Slowing or reducing traffic speed in a specified location, sometimes by physical elements such as speed bumps or restricted lanes.

Turn Signal:

Definition: A device on a vehicle indicating the driver's desire to turn or change lanes.

U

U-Turn:

Definition: A maneuver in which a driver turn the car 180 degrees to go in the other direction.

V

Vehicle Identification Number (VIN):

Definition: A unique alphanumeric number assigned to each car for identification purposes, often placed on the dashboard or driver's side door frame.

Visibility Triangle:

Definition: A clear field of vision at junctions emphasizing the need for unhindered views for safe turning.

W

Work Zone:

Definition: A defined area on the road where construction or repair works are taking place, sometimes indicated by lower speed restrictions and caution signs.

Wrong-Way Driving:

Definition: Driving in the opposing direction of traffic flow on a one-way street or highway.

X

X-Intersection:

Definition: A crossing or intersection of two highways that forms an "X."

Y

Yield:

Definition: To give the right of way to other motorists, usually at an intersection or while merging onto a highway.

Z

Zero Tolerance:

Definition: A stringent regulation prohibiting specific activities, such as driving under the influence, with zero tolerance for any level of infraction.

This comprehensive glossary, organized from A to Z, encompasses a wide range of terminology found in the Massachusetts Driver's Manual. As you navigate the world of driving rules, mastering this language will help you traverse the roads with confidence and adhere to the principles of safe and responsible driving. Happy driving, and may your journeys be smooth and secure!

Practice Tests and Study Tips

Embarking on the journey to obtain your driver's license in Massachusetts requires effective study strategies and comprehensive preparation. Elevate your confidence and competence with these valuable resources designed to enhance your understanding and ensure success in licensing exams.

Practice Tests: Simulating Real Exam Conditions

Official RMV Practice Tests:
- **Source:** [www.mass.gov/rmv]
- **Purpose:** Access the official practice tests provided by the Massachusetts Registry of Motor Vehicles (RMV). These tests replicate the format and content of the actual exams, providing a realistic preview of what to expect.

Online Driving Schools:
- **Source:** Various accredited online driving schools. These driving schools have established a reputation for delivering quality driver's education over the years and are trusted by many for providing top-notch training:

  DriversEd.com

  DriverEdToGo.com

  SafeMotorist.com

CyberEdDriverEd**

Lund's Corner Driving School

These institutions have a track record of excellence and are recognized for their commitment to imparting comprehensive and reliable driver's education. If you have any specific questions about these schools or if there's anything else you'd like assistance with, feel free to ask!

- **Purpose:** Explore practice tests offered by reputable online driving schools. These tests cover a diverse range of topics, ensuring a thorough review of Massachusetts driving regulations.

Mobile Apps:

- **Source:** App stores (iOS and Android)
- **Purpose:** Download mobile apps tailored for driver's license preparation. These apps often feature interactive practice tests, allowing convenient study sessions anytime, anywhere.

Study Tips: Maximizing Your Learning Experience

Understand the Manual:
- **Tip:** Delve into the Massachusetts Driver's Manual, absorbing the rules, regulations, and road signs outlined within. A comprehensive understanding of the manual forms the foundation of your knowledge.

Create a Study Schedule:
- **Tip:** Establish a personalized study schedule that aligns with your routine. Break down the material into manageable sections and allocate specific times for focused review.

Use Flashcards:
- **Tip:** Reinforce key information by creating flashcards covering road signs, rules, and definitions. Flashcards offer a quick and effective method for reviewing essential concepts.

Take Notes:
- **Tip:** While reading the manual, jot down notes on important concepts. The act of writing enhances comprehension and aids in the retention of information.

Visual Aids:
- **Tip:** Utilize visual aids such as diagrams and charts to grasp complex concepts. Visualizing information enhances understanding and facilitates memory recall.

Simulate Exam Conditions:
- **Tip:** During practice tests, replicate exam conditions as closely as possible. Minimize distractions, adhere to time constraints, and analyze your performance to identify areas for improvement.

Focus on Weak Areas:
- **Tip:** Identify and prioritize weak areas revealed during practice tests. Devote additional study time to these topics,

ensuring a targeted approach to enhancing your overall knowledge.

Join Study Groups:
- **Tip:** Consider joining or forming a study group with fellow learners. Engaging in discussions with peers provides diverse perspectives and enriches your understanding of driving concepts.

Stay Updated:
- **Tip:** Stay informed about any updates or changes to Massachusetts driving regulations. Regularly check the official RMV website for announcements to ensure your knowledge is current.

Practice Defensive Driving:
- **Tip:** Apply defensive driving techniques during practice tests. Understanding how to respond in various scenarios is crucial for both the exams and real-world driving situations.

Incorporate these practice tests and study tips into your preparation routine to approach the licensing exams with confidence. Remember, a robust understanding of Massachusetts driving regulations is not only for exam success but for a lifetime of safe and responsible driving. Best wishes on your path to become a licensed driver!

Additional Information: Improve Your Driving Experience

- Use traffic update applications to get real-time information on road conditions, closures, and alternate routes.
- **Community Driving Forums:** Participate in online forums or groups to exchange experiences, advice, and remain updated about local driving issues.
- **Eco-Friendly Driving Practices:** Learn eco-friendly driving behaviors to help protect the environment while on the road.
- **Driver Assistance Programs:** Discover programs for older drivers, novice drivers, and those with particular requirements.

Copyrighted Material

These resources are intended to provide you with comprehensive information, advice, and tools for navigating the changing environment of Massachusetts driving. Whether you're looking for official updates, safety rules, or practical recommendations, these websites and connections can help you become a more educated and responsible driver. Safe travels on Massachusetts highways!

APPENDIX: SAMPLE TEST QUESTIONS

In this section, you will encounter a set of sample questions designed to evaluate your understanding of various aspects of driving in the Massachusetts. Whether you are preparing for a learner's permit or a license exam, these questions encompass both multiple-choice and scenario-based formats, offering a comprehensive assessment of your knowledge. Let's explore:

Multiple-Choice Questions

Traffic Signs:
What does it mean when a circular blue symbol with a white arrow is shown on a traffic sign?
　a. The hospital is located in front of you
　b. There is only one-way traffic
　c. There is a mandatory direction
　d. There is a rest space nearby

Right of Way:

Who has the right of way at a four-way stop sign intersection?

    a. The vehicle that is on the left

    b. The car that comes first

    c. The vehicle that is turning right

    d. The vehicle that has the loudest horn

    e. The vehicle that is facing the other direction

Speed Limits:

What is the normal speed limit in residential areas, regardless of whether or not there is a sign indicating otherwise?

    a. 25 mph

    b. 30 mph

    c. 35 mph

    d. 40 mph

Lane Usage:

What is the function of a solid white line between lanes on the road?

    a. To designate a turn-only lane

    b. To divide traffic traveling in the same direction

c. To assist cars around curves

d. To mark the start of an acceleration lane

Defensive Driving:

What is the main purpose of defensive driving?

a. Arriving at your location as fast as possible

b. Avoiding conflicts with other drivers

c. Anticipating and reacting to potential dangers

d. Ignoring aggressive drivers on the road

Traffic Signals:

What does a solid green traffic signal indicate?

a. Stop

b. Proceed with caution

c. Yield

d. Go, if the route is clear

Pedestrian Crossings:

What does a flashing orange hand signal at a pedestrian crossing mean?

a. Pedestrians may cross

b. Finish crossing quickly

c. Do not cross

d. Proceed with care

Alcohol and Driving:

What impact does alcohol have on driving skills?

    a. Improves concentration

    b. Enhances response time

    c. Impairs judgment and coordination

    d. Increases visibility at night

Road Markings:

What does a double solid yellow line on the road indicate?

    a. Passing is permitted in both directions

    b. No passing permitted in either direction

    c. Passing is permitted in one direction

    d. Passing is permitted with caution

Parking Regulations:

What does a red-painted curb indicate?

    a. Loading zone

    b. No parking or stopping

    c. Short-term parking

    d. Handicapped parking

Scenario-Based Questions

Intersection Dilemma:

Approaching a four-way stop sign simultaneously with another car. To whom does the right of way belong?

    a. The vehicle on the left

    b. The vehicle on the right

    c. The vehicle turning to the left

    d. The vehicle with more passengers

Pedestrian Crossing:

As you approach a designated crosswalk with a pedestrian waiting to cross. What should you do?

    a. Proceed without stopping

    b. Slow down and proceed

    c. Stop and yield the right of way.

    d. Change lanes to avoid the pedestrian

Merge Safely:

You are merging onto a busy highway. What is the best way to enter the flow of traffic?

    a. Come to a full stop before merging

    b. Accelerate swiftly to match the pace of traffic

    c. Merge gently and adapt to the flow

    d. Honk your horn to inform other vehicles

Emergency Vehicle Approach:

An emergency vehicle with lights and sirens is coming from behind. What is the proper action to take?

    a. Stop and move to the right.

    b. Increase your speed to clear the road

    c. Change lanes abruptly

    d. Continue at a steady pace

Adverse Weather Conditions:

You are driving in heavy rain, and visibility is decreased. What precautions should you take?

    a. Use high-beam headlights

    b. Increase your speed for greater control

    c. Use low beam headlights and lower speed

    d. Turn off headlights to prevent glare

Roundabout Navigation:

You approaching a roundabout with many lanes. Which lane should you utilize to make a right turn?

    a. The leftmost lane

b. The middle lane

c. The rightmost lane

d. Any lane, since they all lead to the same exit

School Bus Stop:

A school bus with flashing red lights and an extended stop sign is ahead. What must you do?

a. Pass cautiously on the left

b. Proceed with caution

c. Stop until the lights stop flashing

d. Change lanes and continue

Parallel Parking:

You are parallel parking on a busy roadway. What is the right method to place your car during the maneuver?

a. Angle your car away from the curb

b. Position your vehicle at a 90-degree angle to the curb

c. Angle your vehicle toward the curb

d. Park in the center of the roadway for improved visibility

Handling Road Rage:

Another driver demonstrates aggressive behavior towards you. What is the best course of action?

    a. Respond with hostile gestures

    b. Ignore the conduct and continue driving

    c. Tailgate to demonstrate dominance

    d. Challenge the motorist to a race

Emergency Brake Failure:

Your vehicle's brakes fail unexpectedly. What should you do first?

    a. Pump the brakes repeatedly

    b. Shift to a lower gear

    c. Apply the parking brake gently

    d. Steer to the side of the road and use other ways to slow down

Answers and Explanations

The following are the answers and explanations for the multiple-choice questions:

Traffic Signs:

- **Answer:** c. Mandatory direction

- **Explanation:** A circular blue sign with a white arrow denotes an obligatory direction, urging traffic to go in the given direction.

Right of Way:
- **Answer:** b. The vehicle that arrives first
- **Explanation:** At a four-way stop sign junction, the car that comes first or the one on the right normally has the right of way.

Speed Limits:
- **Answer:** a. 25 mph
- **Explanation:** In residential areas, unless otherwise marked, the average speed restriction is 25 mph.

Lane Usage:
- **Answer:** b. To divide traffic traveling in the same direction
- **Explanation:** A solid white line between lanes on the road is used to segregate cars driving in the same direction.

Defensive Driving:
- **Answer:** c. Anticipating and reacting to possible hazards
- **Explanation:** The basic purpose of defensive driving is to anticipate and react to any risks on the road.

Traffic Signals:
- **Answer:** d. Go, if the path is clear
- **Explanation:** A solid green traffic light signifies that drivers can proceed if the path is clear and safe.

Pedestrian Crossings:
- **Answer:** b. Finish crossing quickly
- **Explanation:** A flashing orange hand signal at a pedestrian crossing implies that pedestrians currently in the crosswalk should complete crossing swiftly, and others should not start.

Alcohol and Driving:
- **Answer:** c. Impairs judgment and coordination

- **Explanation:** Alcohol affects judgment and coordination, making it risky to drive under its influence.

Road Markings:
- **Answer:** b. No passing permitted in any direction
- **Explanation:** A double solid yellow line on the road indicates that passing is not allowed in either direction.

Parking Regulations:
- **Answer:** b. No parking or stopping
- **Explanation:** A red-painted curb often signals prohibited parking or halting.

And here are the answers and explanations for Scenario-Based Questions: Applying Knowledge to Real-World Situations:

Intersection Dilemma:
- **Answer:** b. The car on the right
- **Explanation:** At a four-way stop sign, the vehicle on the right has the right of way if two cars approach simultaneously.

Pedestrian Crossing:
- **Answer:** c. Stop and yield the right of way.
- **Explanation:** When a pedestrian is waiting at a designated crosswalk, you must stop and yield the right of way.

Merge Safely:
- **Answer:** c. Merge gradually and react to the flow
- **Explanation:** When merging onto a congested highway, merge gently, matching the pace of traffic, and adapt to the flow.

Emergency Vehicle Approach:
- **Answer:** a. Stop and move to the right.
- **Explanation:** When an emergency vehicle with lights and sirens approaches, pull over to the right and stop.

Adverse Weather Conditions:
- **Answer:** c. Use low beam headlights and minimize speed

- Explanation: In heavy rain with restricted visibility, use low-beam headlights and lower speed to maximize safety.

Roundabout Navigation:
- **Answer:** c. The rightmost lane
- **Explanation:** When performing a right turn on a roundabout with many lanes, utilize the rightmost lane for a smooth exit.

School Bus Stop:
- **Answer:** c. Stop until the lights stop flashing
- **Explanation:** When a school bus displays flashing red lights and an extended stop sign, you must come to a full stop until the lights stop flashing.

Parallel Parking:
- **Answer:** c. slant your car toward the curb
- **Explanation:** While parallel parking, slant your vehicle toward the curb, keeping a safe distance.

Handling Road Rage:
- **Answer:** b. Ignore the conduct and continue driving

- **Explanation:** The best course of action when dealing with road rage is to maintain cool, disregard aggressive conduct, and continue driving safely.

Emergency Brake Failure:
- **Answer:** d. Steer to the side of the road and utilize alternative ways to slow down
- **Explanation:** In the case of brake failure, steer to the side of the road and utilize other techniques, such as downshifting or the parking brake, to slow down.

CONCLUSION

As we conclude the Massachusetts Driver's Manual 2024, I want to express my heartfelt gratitude to each reader who joined me on this journey toward safer and more responsible driving. My goal has been to equip you with the knowledge necessary to navigate the roads of Massachusetts with confidence.

If this manual has made even a single positive impact on your understanding of driving regulations, road safety, or the nuances of Massachusetts traffic, I consider my mission a success. Your dedication to absorbing these lessons plays a crucial role in our collective effort to create safer roadways for all.

Your words matters, and I urge you to share your thoughts through reviews and feedback. Your experiences, insights, and encouragement act as valuable beacons, guiding others on their path to becoming informed and conscientious drivers. Your words aren't just a review; they are a catalyst for positive change.

Remember, your commitment to responsible driving goes beyond the pages of this manual. Every safe journey, every considerate gesture on the road, and every informed decision contributes to fostering a culture of safety and responsibility.

Thank you for being an integral part of this journey. Your words, whether shared with friends, family, or fellow drivers, stand as a testament to the impact of knowledge in creating a safer driving environment. May your future travels be marked by safety, responsibility, and the shared goal of making our roads a secure space for all.

Safe travels, and thank you for choosing to be a responsible driver.

Best regards,

Heather Adams

Author of the Massachusetts Driver's Manual 2024